"Finally, someone has written a how-to manual for couples striving to achieve equality. *Equally Shared Parenting* is, however, much more than a road map. It is inspirational, insightful, and very well written. It is shot through with the simple yet powerful message that, with enough courage and enough work, love really can conquer the forces of patriarchy."

—Robert Drago, professor of labor studies and women's studies,
Pennsylvania State University, and author of *Striking a Balance*

"Amy and Marc Vachon show us that 'equal parenting' is not an oxymoron. Through their own and others' research, but most of all through their own example, they inspire us to lead the committed and conscious lives that most of us long for—lives with room for our children, our work, our partners, and our selves. Offering real strategies that are pragmatic and flexible, the Vachons walk their talk, and remind us that true gender equality begins at home."

—Pamela Stone, professor of sociology, Hunter College/City University
of New York, and author of *Opting Out?*

"Marc and Amy Vachon have succeeded in becoming absolute parenting partners."

—*The New York Times Magazine*

"Once upon a time, did you dream that family life could be equal, but along the way you gave up? Well, forget the stress-inducing his work/her work 'scorecard' approach, and rev up the equality dream again. With energy, verve, and joy, the Vachons are bringing love and fun back into family life. *Equally Shared Parenting* is an equality guidebook filled to the brim with practical steps and how-tos."

—Miriam Peskowitz, author of *The Truth Behind the Mommy Wars*
and coauthor of *The Daring Book for Girls*

"Rising above the finger-pointing and hand-wringing that all too often pervades the debate about gender and family change, *Equally Shared Parenting* provides a masterful, refreshing, and altogether convincing analysis of the joys, practical steps, and persisting obstacles to sharing—not dividing—caretaking and breadwinning. Amy and Marc Vachon have given us an uplifting blueprint for fashioning more flexible and egalitarian ways of living, loving, and working in the twenty-first century. This is a visionary book that is must-reading for caring couples and policy makers alike."

—Kathleen Gerson, professor of sociology, New York University,
and author of *The Unfinished Revolution*

"[The Vachons are] the Obamas of the parental blogosphere."

—*The Guardian* (UK)

"Marc and Amy Vachon aren't scholars and they aren't journalists. They're ordinary people who are extraordinarily committed to creating a family based on sharing and equality. *Equally Shared Parenting* is a wise, thoughtful blueprint that will help all parents build more balanced and meaningful lives."

—Jeremy Adam Smith, author of *The Daddy Shift* and editor of Shareable.net

continued . . .

"Amy and Marc Vachon have written the book that didn't exist when we plunged enthusiastically into an equal parenting partnership. This must-read shows that, while there's no 'perfect' way to create this life, there are many ways it can work. The Vachons show any couple how to define what needs doing and really share the work and rewards of being a fully engaged parent."

—**Nancy Gruver and Joe Kelly, cofounders of *New Moon Girls* magazine, parenting educators, and authors of *How to Say It to Girls* and *Dads & Daughters***

"Equality and balance are not impossible pipe dreams but real choices for today's couples. The Vachons lead us through all the dilemmas and obstacles that divert dual-earner couples from enjoyable family and work lives and explain step-by-step how to create an equally sharing family, an enriching career, and even a personal life beyond work and family. A call for change, this book brilliantly portrays how much men, as well as women, have to gain from a much-needed revolution in family life."

—**Francine M. Deutsch, professor of psychology, Mount Holyoke College, and author of *Halving It All***

"Decades of social science research have shown that shared parenting can work, but academic articles and books don't convey what it feels like or how to do it. Marc and Amy Vachon's new book fills this void. *Equally Shared Parenting* is packed full of compelling personal stories about how the next generation of couples is reinventing parenting and modern marriage, and provides the 'nuts and bolts' of shared parenting. The advice they offer about how to balance family and work is indispensible for new parents. Highly recommended."

—**Scott Coltrane, dean, College of Arts and Sciences, University of Oregon, and author of *Family Man* and *Gender and Families***

"In the '60s, many people understood that for women to achieve equality at work they would need to achieve equality at home. In most families that hasn't happened yet, and not so surprisingly when you look at the data there is a profound bias against mothers in hiring, wages, and career advancement. Equally shared parenting is a wonderful movement that is working to free parents to realize equality at home not because it is good for women but because it is a joyful alternative."

—**Joan Blades, cofounder of MomsRising.org and MoveOn.org**

"Want to learn how to divide childcare, housework, and moneymaking responsibilities without falling into stereotypical 'Mommy' and 'Daddy' roles? Then follow the advice in *Equally Shared Parenting* and watch yourself, your marriage, and your children flourish."

—**Monique Tilford, coauthor of *Your Money or Your Life*, and Dave Tilford, senior writer for Center for a New American Dream**

EQUALLY SHARED
PARENTING

Rewriting the Rules for
a New Generation of Parents

Marc and Amy Vachon

A PERIGEE BOOK

A PERIGEE BOOK
Published by the Penguin Group
Penguin Group (USA) Inc.
375 Hudson Street, New York, New York 10014, USA
Penguin Group (Canada), 90 Eglinton Avenue East, Suite 700, Toronto, Ontario M4P 2Y3, Canada
(a division of Pearson Penguin Canada Inc.)
Penguin Books Ltd., 80 Strand, London WC2R 0RL, England
Penguin Group Ireland, 25 St. Stephen's Green, Dublin 2, Ireland (a division of Penguin Books Ltd.)
Penguin Group (Australia), 250 Camberwell Road, Camberwell, Victoria 3124, Australia
(a division of Pearson Australia Group Pty. Ltd.)
Penguin Books India Pvt. Ltd., 11 Community Centre, Panchsheel Park, New Delhi—110 017, India
Penguin Group (NZ), 67 Apollo Drive, Rosedale, North Shore 0632, New Zealand
(a division of Pearson New Zealand Ltd.)
Penguin Books (South Africa) (Pty.) Ltd., 24 Sturdee Avenue, Rosebank, Johannesburg 2196,
South Africa

Penguin Books Ltd., Registered Offices: 80 Strand, London WC2R 0RL, England

While the author has made every effort to provide accurate telephone numbers and Internet addresses
at the time of publication, neither the publisher nor the author assumes any responsibility for errors, or
for changes that occur after publication. Further, the publisher does not have any control over and
does not assume any responsibility for author or third-party websites or their content.

Copyright © 2010 by Marc Vachon and Amy Vachon
Text design by Ellen Cipriano

First edition: January 2010

Library of Congress Cataloging-in-Publication Data

Vachon, Marc, 1963–
Equally shared parenting : rewriting the rules for a new generation of parents / Marc and
Amy Vachon.— 1st ed.
p. cm.
Includes bibliographical references and index.
ISBN 978-0-399-53558-1
1. Parenting. 2. Sex role. 3. Dual-career families. I. Vachon, Amy. II. Title.
HQ755.8.V32 2010
306.872—dc22 2009041110

PRINTED IN THE UNITED STATES OF AMERICA

10 9 8 7 6 5 4 3 2 1

To Maia and Theo—we love you a thousand million.

CONTENTS

PART
THREE
Navigating
the Barriers

FOREWORD

Lisa Belkin, *New York Times* reporter

Amy and Marc Vachon, two laid-back and loving parents living in a house with a white picket fence outside of Boston, are doing what years of feminism, workplace reform, gender-equality laws, sniping between the sexes, and best intentions of spouses have not: They are living as parenting equals.

An anecdotal look around shows how far we have to go. Run through a mental list of couples that you know; I'll wager that most default their family's childcare and housework to the wife. Then scan the shelves of books out there for new parents; you'll find that most assume their readers are mothers, and that balance, nap schedules, and playdate logistics are Mom's problem, with Dad mentioned as "helping," if he's mentioned at all.

Want data rather than anecdote? Any way you measure it, women do about twice as much around the house as men. The National Survey of Families and Households shows that more than four decades after Betty Friedan, the average wife does thirty-one hours of housework a week, while the average husband does fourteen—a ratio of slightly more than two to one. If you break out couples in which wives stay home and husbands are the sole earners, the number of hours goes up for women, to thirty-eight hours of housework a week, and down a bit for men, to twelve, a ratio of more than three to one. That makes sense because the couples have defined home as one partner's work.

But then break out the couples in which both husband and wife have full-time paying jobs. In those cases, the wife does twenty-eight hours of housework and the husband, sixteen. Just shy of two to one, which makes no sense at all.

On to childcare. Here the ratio is more like five to one and, as with housework, does not change as much as you might expect when you account for who brings home a paycheck. In a family in which Mom stays home and Dad goes to work, she spends fifteen hours a week caring for children, and he spends two. In families in which both parents are wage earners, Mom's average drops to eleven and Dad's goes up to three. Lest you think this is at least a significant improvement over our parents and grandparents, not so fast. It's pretty much the same ratio as it was ninety years ago.

That would be fine, of course, if everyone in all those lopsided couples was happy, but anecdotal evidence certainly suggests that they aren't, and there are data to document that discontent as well. (Some 58 percent of women say the division of labor in modern families is not fair to them, and that who does what is at the top of the list of things couples fight about; need I go on?)

A few years ago, I set out to write an article for the *New York Times Magazine* exploring why a setup that makes no sense is so entrenched, and what it would take—an overhaul of the economy? of biology?—to bring about change. That's when I met Marc and Amy, who are dynamic proof of the fact that no external overhaul is necessary. Instead, what is needed are some changes inside our homes and inside ourselves.

What Amy and Marc hit on was that the status quo is not just unfair to women—it is equally unfair to men. Yes, it shoehorns women into a place where they are considered the primary parent, but in doing so, it relegates men, just as firmly, into the secondary role, a sort of deputy. Yes, it forces women to feel they must sacrifice career for family, but that simultaneously forces men to feel that bringing home a paycheck is primarily their burden. It leaves spouses feeling like opponents rather than partners, combatants rather than a team.

The solution, Marc and Amy believe, means looking at family life as a shared whole, where things are about equal—equal hours spent at work, equal time spent with children, equal energy spent on housework, equal responsibility for the mental checklists (the dog needs a checkup or the baby needs new shoes, etc.). It means the benefits are equal, too—free time for the gym or dinner with a friend, and feelings of connection with your children plus feelings of liberation from "the all" of anything.

This probably requires changing how you view work—seeing it as something you can leave behind when you aren't working, rather than something that consumes you whenever you are awake. And it probably requires changing how you view home. You have to accept that your partner won't do things exactly the way you might, and that has to be okay, because when it is their turn, it is completely their turn, or you aren't really sharing equally.

Amy and Marc will describe the details in the pages that follow. Before they do, I would like to leave you with two thoughts:

First, this is not for everyone. Some couples are completely happy with whatever imbalance they've built into their lives because it suits their personalities or their professional goals. If both of you are content with the equation, then that is a kind of balance. But I'd bet those aren't the kinds of couples who have picked up this book.

Second, this is not about keeping score. That was the question I heard most often after I wrote about Marc and Amy: How can they stand such a regimented/list-driven/micromanaged life?

When you are with them, you see that what they have is precisely the opposite of all that. They have crafted a life such that they have one conversation about who will do what, they make a list every once in a while, and then they don't have to discuss it again—because they trust that their spouse has it covered.

They laugh a lot. They are strikingly relaxed most of the time. And they hold hands like newlyweds. That alone should be enough to make you want to find out how it works.

INTRODUCTION

Back when we were expecting our first child, the idea of becoming parents was both wonderful and frightening. On one hand, we were elated, amazed, and deeply grateful as we anticipated taking the plunge. But on the other, we each silently wondered, *What have I done to my life?*

All around us, coworkers, friends, family members, and media pundits talking and writing about early parenthood were trumpeting the misery of this life-changing state. It seemed like every parent in the world was ready to testify that after a baby arrives, your own personal happy, fun, enjoyable, sane, and rested life was over. You'll be lucky to take a shower or do a load of laundry. Your greatest wish will be to sleep—and it won't be granted for eighteen years. You'll always want to be at home when you're at work and at work when you're home. And forget about ever going to the bathroom in peace again. Yes, most of these predictions spoke primarily to new mothers. But new fathers, too, seemed to be burdened with the responsibility of providing materially for their growing families while missing out on much of the joy of parenthood. Experts further warned that a baby was a menace to your very relationship—destroying your sex life and your mutual happiness. This doomsday scenario made such an impression on us that we became determined to find a way to beat it. We vowed to sidestep what the world expected new parents to be—bleary-eyed, short-tempered, lonely, and isolated.

The strategy that came to us in small moments of clarity over the ensuing months was to share everything—the good and the bad—together. We would be *peers* in this great adventure, not just in the overall sense but in each significant area of parenthood—in caring for our baby, in handling the housework, and in bringing in the paychecks. We would also make sure we each had enough time for our own personal brands of fun, and time to be together. Our goal was to preserve ourselves while we made room for a baby—carving out enough from our former lives but not so much that either of us lost what matters most. We would share the burdens so that nothing would consistently overwhelm either of us, and share the joys so that neither missed out on the experience of a deep connection with our child. Our *daughter*, as we soon learned.

Decorating her room, buying her vast supplies, and learning about her physical care were the easy parts. The tougher work came as we battened down our marriage against her winds as best as a still child-free couple could. Our growing stack of pregnancy and childcare books held not a word on how to share equally in raising a child. We then searched self-help books, websites, anything. With few exceptions, the voice that surfaced was complaining—complaining about the burdens and pressures of motherhood, fathers who don't do their part, or the need for legislative change to support families. "Don't worry," we tried to reassure each other, "this is common sense. We can do it."

When our baby girl—Maia—finally arrived, we were as euphoric as any new parents. And immediately became bleary-eyed as predicted. But slowly, over the next few months, we put our homegrown plan into effect. What a crazy trip it is to become someone's parent—to have a tiny stranger suddenly appear and then become yours to nurture and protect! Everything was surreal, from breastfeeding to stroller walks to watching her sweet face as she slept. We mucked our way through wails, baths, diapers, nap routines, preemie weight checks, and lead scares. Determined not to be derailed in our partnership by the usual pitfalls, we took turns at everything. Breast milk was saved in freezer bags to allow for shared feeding responsibilities. All skills—from clipping fingernails to treating diaper rash—were learned by both of us. We coordinated our duties to make sure each of us got a shift of uninterrupted sleep every night. With each shared task, our enjoyment seemed to deepen as we both became more practiced at our new skills and relaxed a bit.

We took advantage of leave policies at our companies to carve out time for both of us with Maia. Maternity leave was extended to about four months (using sick and vacation time with the remainder unpaid) from Amy's job as a clinical pharmacist, while Marc's IT technical consultant position gave him two weeks of paid paternity leave that he further stretched by taking carefully saved vacation time on Tuesdays and Thursdays for three months. It wasn't absolutely equal yet, but the arrangement gave us a legitimate run at coparenting rather than the usual primary mother and understudy father roles. With both of us loitering around the house together three to four days a week, we began to look at each other and grin. Neither of us was tired or overwhelmed! "This is the life," we told ourselves.

With things going fairly well at home, we lifted our heads and took a look around. Were others living this way? Where were they? We set out to find them. The first stop was a new mothers' group for Amy. Surely someone in this circle of women nursing their well-dressed babies would want to discuss the joys and challenges of equal sharing.

"My husband is worthless when the baby starts crying."

"Mine isn't around enough for me to find out."

"I would never ask him to get up at night—he needs his sleep so he can go to work."

This didn't sound good. Was optimum alertness really more crucial at work than at home, day after day? And why all the man bashing? Almost every mother in this group had quit her job to stay home with her baby. We felt a mixture of gratitude and old fear: that could have been us, but thankfully it wasn't.

Undaunted, we both joined a new parents' group. With fathers in the room, we figured we'd have more luck meeting some equal-minded couples. Strike two. They were all nice people, but in every situation it was clear that Mom was in charge, and she was really, really tired. The dads deferred to their spouses in almost every baby decision that was discussed and seemed to be trying to helpfully stay out of the way. Finally Amy found a local *working* mothers' group. These moms, it turned out, were closer to our peers—and warmly welcoming—with an emphasis on seeking some degree of balance. Yet when Amy first met them, their discussion centered around doing so independently, without much talk of how their husbands could figure into the equation.

Finding no fathers' groups in the area, Marc was relegated to chatting with men on the playground. While he met plenty of men who enjoyed time with their children, and even some who stayed home with them, he did not find any fathers who shared all aspects of family life equally with their partners.

Meanwhile, our leaves and vacation time ran out. Summoning our negotiation skills, the precedence of colleagues, our personal seniority and past performance ratings, and a bit of courage, we approached our bosses to request permanent reduced-hour work-weeks. It was a combination of savvy and luck that won a "yes" from each. We both secured work schedules at about thirty hours per week with prorated benefits, with overlap on only Mondays and Wednesdays. An eighteen-hour-per-week spot for our daughter at our neighbor's family daycare completed the picture.

Our days were not all smooth. Styles of parenting clashed, classic expectations of fatherhood and motherhood haunted us and had to be reasoned with, and budgets had to be reined in to accommodate our new incomes. But these things were bearable. Our lives seemed in balance rather than stressed to capacity, and we each felt like we were getting the best of all worlds. Our faith in equal parenting grew even stronger.

And so it went as Maia grew to toddlerhood, and then we started the process over again. With the arrival of our son, Theo, nearly three years later, we once again searched for peers and experts, any guiding voices from whom we could learn or with whom we could share our experiences. Books, blogs, and magazine articles fashionably described, in intimate detail, the secret lives of mothers who were crushed under the weight of their drudgery, anxiety, and loneliness—not just during the first few months or even years of parenting but for decades to come. "Why didn't anyone tell me how bad it would be?" had become a common cry. It was as if "the problem that has no name," described in 1963 by Betty Friedan in *The Feminine Mystique*, which referred to the empty lives of women as subservient homemakers, had resurfaced as the unbearable lives of women as modern-day mothers.

As we read these tales—even stronger versions of what we'd read and feared before we became parents ourselves—our frustration built. Yes, these stories had an important message to share. True, it is useful to bring isolation and overburden out into the open for discussion. But why stop there? Did women really have to settle for these miserable lives? And how come no one was mentioning *fathers*? The pain in this literature was almost palpable, and yet we knew it didn't have to be this way. Without a doubt, many family situations can make life extremely difficult—such as single parenthood or the serious mental or physical illness of one parent. But in a home with two loving and capable parents, "Why didn't anyone tell me?" had a different meaning to us: why wasn't anyone talking about *both parents sharing the burdens and joys*?

Over the next few years, we did find others like us. Someone knew a neighbor whose friend "does the equal sharing thing" or a young mother or father heard our story and said "us, too—and we thought we were the only ones." We were particularly excited to find the ThirdPath Institute, a nonprofit organization dedicated to helping people redesign work and life—with an emphasis on sharing the load between partners. But beyond this, there was still no public conversation about this way of life. By the time Theo was eating solids, we knew we had to speak up.

...

In 2006, we dug into hammering out the principles of this lifestyle for others to read. We chose a name for it—"equally shared parenting"—based on a term used by Francine Deutsch, a social psychologist at Mount Holyoke College who studies parents like us (she even runs her own "ESP lab"). Other names have been used in sociology or business publications to describe this concept, including "egalitarian marriage," "peer parenting" and "shared care," but our choice was based on what we felt was most descriptive on its own. We also established a definition for this family model that widened its scope beyond simply parenting:

Equally shared parenting is the purposeful practice of two parents sharing equally in the four domains of *childraising*, *breadwinning*, *housework*, and *time for self*.

Even more important than this definition, we outlined the underlying goal of this lifestyle:

Equally shared parenting aims to create an *equal partnership* between parents and an *individually balanced life* for each.

Later that year, we went public by launching the website EquallySharedParenting.com. We were about to find out what the outside world thought of this lifestyle. Critics weighed in over the first year, giving us a mental workout as they tested our ideas—and helping us refine them. More equally sharing couples found us and expressed their delight in finally having a name for the life they were carefully tending. Professionals in the fields of sociology, psychology, and work/life balance lent support to our theories and agreed that no one to date had adequately described the practicalities of an equal marriage with children. We reached out to, and began to get attention from, parenting blogs across the country. And then one day we received a little email from Lisa Belkin, a leading work/life balance journalist for the *New York Times*. Her message was simply titled, "We have to talk."

What began in such a small way became a ten-page cover article in the *New York Times Sunday Magazine* on Father's Day 2008 and a video of our lives on *The TODAY Show*. Overnight, we became the poster couple for equally shared parenting, and the whole world seemed to be talking. Together with Lisa and others covered in her story, we had succeeded in starting the discussion that we were so amazed had not begun before this. It was a dream come true. Mission accomplished?

We received many wonderful messages from like-minded parents who were excited to see such media space devoted to this topic. And from young parents-to-be who were thankful for a bit of hope for the years ahead . . . that the life they feared would not necessarily have to become their reality. But we soon realized that not everyone was getting it. We read many comments and subsequent follow-up blogs and news articles that didn't describe our life. One frequent comment went something like, "What's so special about that?" Another flatly cut off the idea by stating, "There is no such thing as equally shared parenting." We were accused of having a business-like marriage, harming our children, and nitpicking each other over every chore. A nerve had been hit, people's defenses were up, and the dichotomy was deafening. We started to appreciate that this lifestyle needed a lot of explaining— more than could be derived from a few snippets on a weblog or one exposé in the news. We knew equal sharing was neither common nor impossible, and that these misconceptions did not come close to capturing the reality of couples living this way. Our lifestyle had its own challenges, but these were not them. There was so much more to say!

It is now over seven years since our daughter's birth, and what started as a personal mission to sidestep the plunge into chaos described for most new parents became a deeply important way of life for us. It then widened into a passion to bring equally shared parenting to the consciousness of all parents through our website and now this book. What you are reading is the culmination of our mission to give equally shared parenting its rightful place at the table of lifestyle options. It is our way of injecting good news into the global parenting discussion amid all the negativity.

Into this book we pour all our experience and philosophies of equal parenting, and those of many other couples we've interviewed who live this way, so that we can give you practical steps that make it work for *you*. We also include, we hope, a bit of cheerleading, knowing that courage is needed whenever one strays from the standard life. This book has been written by both of us equally. Using many of the principles of equally shared parenting, we sometimes worked simultaneously, sometimes separately, always using our individual strengths and supporting each other's weaknesses. We switched off roles as writer, big-picture thinker, interviewer, detail gatherer, and first-pass editor, and we're both fully invested in the life we share openly with you.

Writing about such a personal topic—how parents run a home and raise their children together—is bound to engender emotions on all sides. We know this, and that there is no way around it. Our mission is not to safely author a cookbook of 101 brownie recipes, but neither is it to judge any set of parents. So despite the fact that we contrast equal sharing with more standard parenting lifestyles in several chapters, this book is not intended as a debate in which equally shared parenting "wins." Trying to convince anyone to adopt any specific family model is a worthless endeavor—this is just too heartfelt a choice to be made by logical argument. This love story with equally shared parenting, then, is written for an audience of its admirers. We invite you to join us as we lay out the joys and challenges of this life. And in the end, we hope you, too, discover that "parenthood," "happy life," and "intimate partnership" are compatible realities.

PART ONE

SETTING THE FOUNDATION

When two people love each other, shouldn't it be natural for them to live and parent together as equals? Just draw up a set of ground rules for sharing the lullabies and the laundry, and you and your beloved can live equally (and happily) ever after! Yet you know it's not quite that simple. What might seem intuitive in theory is not so in practice.

If you're like most of us, equally shared parenting is not a way of life that your parents taught or modeled for you. So, before you can claim it for yourself—before you can be expected to smooth out mundane details like who changes that dirty diaper, who is leaving work early to pick up the kids today, who's cooking tonight's dinner, or who gets to sleep in on Saturday—it is important to first understand what such a relationship might look like. Your personally guided tour starts in the next chapter.

Once you have a clear picture of this lifestyle, the second step is determining whether or not it matches your values. Is it the right life for *you? for your partner? You can do this by taking a careful look at its two philosophical foundations—*equality *(an equal partnership) and* balance *(individually balanced lives). The subsequent pair of chapters is dedicated to examining each of these foundations.*

Equally shared parenting is fully possible, but it is neither a quick fix nor an unplanned sure thing. Embracing its philosophies comes first, with its practice more naturally following after. And so that is how we, too, will begin.

1

Welcome to the Possibility

It is no secret that raising a child can be a wild ride and often provides us with our greatest joys and challenges. Each day and each stage is a new adventure. But step back from considering the daily ups and downs for a minute. Think more about the big picture of your role as a parent, a partner, a worker. A person. Given the fact that you know it won't be full of joy and sunshine every day, what would you wish for yourself?

In formal interviews and informal chats over the past five years, we have posed this question to many young women and men who genuinely desire to be parents. Single, married, expecting their first child, or with babe in arms—their answers overlap and echo each other. The wishes and fears of the women we've spoken with tend to be a bit different than those of the men, although not always.

Here is a sampling of what women often say:

- I want to be a mother—to love and cherish my child. But I don't want to lose myself in the process. I'm worried about how my life will work with a child.

- I want to keep my career—to still connect with that part of me that is a successful lawyer/nurse/graphic designer (or fill in the blank). But I don't want my baby in daycare the whole week while I'm working (or for some women, in any daycare at all).

- I don't want my husband to have more power in our relationship just because as a mother I'm supposed to have the less important career (or none at all).

- I'm scared that when I become a mother, I'll forevermore be someone's servant and be burdened with the brunt of childcare—and I'll grow to resent that my life has turned into endless days of chores.

- I want my partner to love being with our child just as much as I do.

- I don't want to carry the full weight of all the decisions about raising a child—I want help with this!

- I want to hold on to something just for me—my own special hobby or passion that doesn't get pushed aside because there's no longer any time to breathe.

- I want to be able to sleep—enough.

- I don't want a baby to come between me and my partner—if anything, I want parenthood to draw us closer as a couple.

- I want to be happy; I want my partner to be happy.

And this is how men often respond to the same question:

- I want to make sure we have enough money to live comfortably with another mouth to feed.

- I don't want to be stuck with all the stress of bringing in the money for the next thirty years, forever working late trying to get the next promotion or avoid the next round of layoffs.

- I want to be a father who knows his children far better than my father knew me as a child.

- I don't want my sex life to tank.

- I'm ready for the challenge of fatherhood, but I still want to have fun. I want to be able to do things I enjoy without feeling guilty or being made to feel guilty.

- I want a fun partner who loves her life, too. I don't want her to always be tired, angry, or frustrated.

- I don't want my life at home to be reduced to checking off my wife's to-do lists; I want to *want* to come home each day.

- I'm afraid that I'll get pushed aside when the baby comes, or I'll get bossed around and told how to take care of the baby or what I'm doing wrong all the time.

- I want to be happy; I want my partner to be happy.

You may want some of these same things as a parent, or have some of the same fears. We certainly did! Statistics mirror the answers we've received, too, across all types of people in their twenties and thirties.[1] But when we look around, what we see is typically very different from what our young respondents say they want. Even today, after all that feminism has fought for, most women still *do* have to make the tough decision between career and family—often either significantly scaling back their careers or dropping out of work—while men generally never give this a thought. Men *do* get marginalized at home and take much of their identities from their jobs instead. Women *are* saddled with far more of the housework and the mundane childcare, while men swoop in for the Fun Daddy Hour but miss thousands of poignant little moments. Men *are* burdened with the responsibility of earning the bulk of the family's income. Couples *do* tend to divide and conquer once a baby arrives, and can drift apart as a result. Power imbalances—both financial and parental—can set in and erode satisfaction for both partners. Each can end up feeling alone much of the time—lonely, tired, and often resentful. And at least one parent usually loses out on a cherished hobby or enough space for personal renewal.

When we talk with parents in traditional relationships about how they ended up where they did—and what frustrates them most—

they often blame the facts. Careers that won't accommodate a baby and so have to be abandoned or chosen at the expense of family time. Financial influences that push one partner into a job with extensive travel and the other into full-time childcare despite their wish to share these duties. Cultural taboos that make men eschew paternity leave and women take control of the nurturing duties. The all-consuming bonds of motherhood. These are some of the many forces that can cause couples to stray from their original vision. Then, there's the contribution of everyday minutiae—bills must be paid, the baby must be fed and rocked, someone has to learn how to give him a bath. Only women can breastfeed. Dad's up for a promotion that will uproot the family but is such a *great* opportunity. Mom's job has a forty-five-minute commute. The baby has colic. Mom gets pregnant again.

Couples on the verge of parenthood, at the very time when life calls on them to stay the course of their dreams, tend to bury their heads in the details of a new baby and just try to survive. They can give up easily and unconsciously, forfeiting their wishes to a life that the world has picked out for them instead. Of course Dad's job offer can't be ignored. Clearly Mom has become so much better at calming the baby's cries. Mom's salary barely pays for childcare. How could we consider handing our precious baby to someone else all day? Dad doesn't know the right way to buy groceries/do the laundry/burp the baby (or you name it). It seems not only easier but even the nobler option to resign to standard gender roles and give up on the dream—for a few years at least. Right?

Granted, we're talking in sweeping generalities here. Many couples are (or appear to be) satisfied with traditional parenting roles. And many others have found ways to scrape away at the worst of their fears and have settled into a semitraditional solution that feels reasonable to both partners. Perhaps she gets permission from her boss to work from home two days a week instead of dropping to part-time or quitting entirely. Maybe he really pitches in at home each evening and on the weekends, and loves being an involved dad. Maybe he takes an extra week of paternity leave when the baby comes. Or they have regular weekly date nights together to preserve their couple time. Or he stays home with the kids and she works—flipping the fears and advantages of each role to the opposite gender. Each of these solutions helps ease the pressure of making room for a precious baby in already busy lives. For some couples, these are enough to sustain them long term. But for many, these options get them only part of the way to real fulfillment.

What would it take to get *all* the way to the kind of life desired by our young interviewees? Let us introduce you to a couple who forged a new path together.

A Shared Vision

Marci and David fell in love on a vacation in Italy. Marci is an architect who managed a busy design firm at the time; she had followed her lawyer father's lead, choosing to work hard in a largely self-directed career. David is a web designer who knew from his early teens that he wanted a *different* life than his father—a man who spent decades commuting a long distance to work in silent misery and having little control over his time. When Marci and David met on that fateful Italian trip—a group vacation coordinated by a mutual friend—they clicked instantly.

As they dated, planned a wedding, and moved David across

the Atlantic from his home in England to their current home in Santa Fe, New Mexico, they had a chance to understand better why they connected so well. Neither wanted a life that centered on the standard American Dream—the possessions and social status that are emblematic of success and unconsciously direct so many of our decisions. As David described their core desire, "We mostly just wanted to be equals. To support each other fully—emotionally, practically, financially. To know that neither of us was more important. That neither of us had dreams or passions that would trump the other's." In Marci's words, "We wanted to be best friends."

This couple put words to their core desires for a life together—words many of us might believe as well. David told Marci that he wanted a life with room for what was most important to him; he didn't want work to consume him completely. Marci explained to David that she expected to hold on to her career, but she, too, was ready to let go of the importance that work played in her identity. She wanted a more well-rounded life now. And she wanted a partner—a true partner—to share it all with her. By voicing their expectations and priorities, David and Marci came to realize that what they both wanted was a relationship based on *equality* and *balance*. It didn't yet have a name or any role models to follow, but it consisted of fully sharing in all that it takes to raise a family, keep a home, earn the money, and enjoy life. And enough time for the things that counted.

Young couples often succeed handily in living this dream—for a while—without even doing much planning. But for many, their equal partnership and balanced lives don't seem to last. Especially once they become parents. Their dream is typically not shaped into a mutual commitment. For some, it is not even discussed aloud. Marci and David's clear vision, communication, and dedication, on the other hand, gave this couple the foresight to forge ahead.

Going the Distance

With parenthood on the horizon, Marci and David's first weapon against an erosion of their equal sharing was to have Marci join David among the ranks of the self-employed. Marci resigned from her architectural firm, and they rented a little downtown office space together with a third business owner. When their baby daughter, Finn, was born two years later, they put the rest of their plan into action. They both made arrangements to take an equivalent amount of time away from work in the early months to be home as a family. They quickly developed a routine for cohandling Finn's needs so that they both got enough sleep. Both of them kept up a small amount of work from home so that they remained in touch with their clients. Then, over the next few months, they ramped up their client loads until they were both working twenty hours per week in the office and extra hours in the evenings as needed.

Marci pumped breast milk for David to feed Finn while she went to work; David handed Finn back to Marci for breastfeeding and care when he headed to the office. They divided their days in half and set up a schedule of when each of them worked mornings versus afternoons. At noon, they met to pass Finn between them. At night, they each cooked about as often, and traded off having time to play with their daughter and get her tucked into bed. They shared housework as well, and although there was no strict division of tasks, neither could say that one of them was doing more than the other. As time went on, David added his most closely valued hobbies back into his life—photography and bicycling (often with baby Finn along). And Marci returned to teaching a spinning class at her gym, in addition to getting in her own workouts and a monthly massage. For the next three years, Finn was cared for exclusively by her two parents.

As they approached parenthood, this couple had the same questions and opportunities that many of us have for how to structure a family. But instead of following tradition, they placed their desire to remain peers and enjoy their lives together above other priorities. Marci and David's resulting life together as parents allows for much, if not all, of the wishes expressed by the men and women at the beginning of this chapter. While they had to make time for all the work of caring for a baby, no adult identities were lost. Two careers, rather than just one, were scaled back but still kept fully meaningful, and outside childcare requirements were minimized (in this case, to zero). Neither partner ended up with more power in the relationship, in terms of either finances or household management. Both shared the joys and the routine responsibilities of childcare every day, relieving each other for time away from endless chores. Both adored being with their daughter and shared all the decision making around her care. And both kept precious hobbies, slept enough, and grew closer for becoming parents together. This couple found a way to assure a strong and intimate father-child bond right from the start, and relieved either parent from more than half of the breadwinning burden. Neither partner felt guilty about taking time for personal fun. Together, they made enough money to sustain the family.

David and Marci had created a life of equally shared parenting.

Owning the Dream

When first hearing of equally shared parenting (or ESP for short), people may wonder why it is any different from the standard family. Don't most husbands pull their weight at home these days? Aren't most women working? Yes, burdens are shared in many families now, but still in unequal ways and not often with balanced lives as a result. Women still typically manage the home and do far more housework and routine childcare than do men. Men still generally define themselves as the primary breadwinners, even if both partners work full-time, and rarely alter their work in any substantial way when children arrive, except when gender roles are reversed.

With equally shared parenting, all these burdens are jointly owned, day in and day out. In fact, when it comes to ESP, "ownership" is a key word. Not only must both partners own a fair share of the housework and childraising duties as well as the responsibility to tend a career, but they must own—as we will explore in detail in the coming chapters—their competence at household chores and managing the needs of the kids. In striving for an individually balanced life for each partner, we also need to own the responsibility for saying no (or yes) so that our work doesn't take over the time we'd rather spend with our kids, with each other, or on our own rejuvenation. We must work within the constraints of the outside world—laws, bosses, social and financial expectations—to claim the lives we want without waiting for the process to become easy. But ownership is far from just "musts" and "need to's." There is immense joy in owning our choices and in experiencing the rewards that they bring.

So if ESP isn't yet common, then is its goal *too* hard to attain by most couples? Are Marci and David just an anomaly, with the perfect setup to live this way? We all know such an arrangement is not effortless or trouble free. In this book, you'll learn where the going typically gets rough for couples who aspire to share all of life's domains. You might have already correctly guessed that this lifestyle requires a high level of trust, respect, and daily communication, and that it takes a certain determination and some risk taking to bypass standard gender roles or societal norms. But you may be surprised to find out that the barriers you think are cast in iron can crumble when you are both ready to let them go.

Don't worry. You needn't cut your weekly work in half or share an office (or even have an office) or be self-employed or have only one child to embrace ESP. This life is possible even if *your* life is nothing like David and Marci's. All ESP couples figure out their own method of balancing their lives and relating to each other as equal partners in all domains of their family. Some, like Marci and David, start out sharing everything from the moment their babies are born. Others rebuild their relationships toward ESP after years of traditional parenting arrangements. Some work in well-paid professional fields with high flexibility; others hold down blue-collar jobs. Many work reduced hours, yet others retain their full-time careers. Their solutions are unique, but the foundations are similar for ESP couples of all stripes and colors. In this book, we will share with you what we've learned about how to make ESP happen and keep it alive—from our own experience and from the stories of many other couples who have reached for it, have found their balance points, and would never choose to live any other way.

There is only one requirement for equally shared parenting: *two willing partners.* Once you know you both want the dream of an equal partnership and balanced lives, just as David and Marci discovered they did, we will show you that the rest is possible. We'll also describe the challenges and sacrifices involved in creating this dream—as no parenting lifestyle is without them.

ESP does not turn on the wind; it is not obliterated the minute one of you no longer has the perfect work schedule, nor is it negated by two partners with different paychecks, different standards for housework, or different ideas about how to raise children. It isn't limited to people with a specific job or maternity or paternity leave benefit, or with better childcare options, a maid, a grandmother living next door, or something else that you don't have. You don't need to wait for the perfect global economic climate or governmental family law changes or family-friendly corporate policies to attain it. You don't need more money. The two of you—with awareness and personal determination—are enough.

Let's Make a Few Things Perfectly Clear

Before we get into the details of ESP's foundations in the next two chapters, please allow us to share a few ground rules for the rest of the book.

As everyday practitioners of ESP, we write from our hearts and experience. This book is a practical guide, *not* an academic text. You will not read lots of statistics or see graphs of raw data or learn about the many studies that support this lifestyle. We have left this important work to others and direct you to some of the key literature in "Additional Reading" at the back of the book. We know that personal decisions are not made by comparing oneself with population trends. And so our job is simply to make equal parenting real—real enough that you can choose it for yourself.

"Don't show that to my wife," say some men who learn what we've been writing. In our conversations with parents of both genders, it is common for them to initially suppose ESP means getting men to pick up their slack. So much is written about the lousy father who doesn't do his share around the house! No fear— we'll not add to this literature, and we vow to crush the myth that browbeating or tricking or guilting men into equality will come to any lasting good. In fact, we will challenge women to face their part in creating unequal relationships. ESP is not a call for men to do more. "We love living this way," says one ESP dad who speaks for many. "No need at all to drag us into it." Most men who earnestly and knowingly sign up for equal sharing do so because it individually appeals to them, not because it is their duty. They know that ESP gives them a full partner in earning the family's income, an authentic daily connection with their kids, equal say in how their household runs, and guilt-free time to themselves—to name a few incentives. And even those who may begin ESP with a sense of obligation end up guarding it fiercely because they get from it as much as women do.

Throughout the book, we generally refer to parents as "husband and wife" or "he and she." We also often direct specific recommendations toward the gender that would stereotypically find them applicable. This is not meant to exclude unmarried parents, same-sex parents, other nontraditional families, or specific men and women who don't hold classic gendered attitudes. We hope you will be able to translate our standard language to fit your family type. We also focus primarily on equal sharing in intact families, rather than shared childraising for divorced parents.

ESP is not a method of *parenting*. We're going to make an assumption that you and your partner are perfectly capable of being good parents—not those nonexistent *perfect* parents but the best parents for *your* child. ESP makes no value judgments about fit parenthood, prescribes no specific methods of discipline, advocates neither for attachment parenting nor cry-it-out sleep solutions. There are strong theoretical benefits to children raised in an ESP home, which we include in our discussion, but we stay away from teaching you how to be a parent.

Finally, this is not an all-or-none book. In the end, we know that every parent needs to figure out how to raise children; feed, shelter, and clothe them; and earn the money needed to do so. ESP is but one of the options available to all of us. And so our wish in writing this book is that each reader can find what works best for his or her life. Together, as a couple, you can decide whether the answer is equally shared parenting, a small piece of ESP, a piece today and maybe more in the future, or something else entirely. Our hope is that your choice is made with open eyes and an understanding of the possibilities.

The "Typical" ESP Family

Parents who practice equal sharing fit many different categories. Some build this lifestyle together specifically because they believe it is the best option for a child, and others come to it because it makes them happy parents, partners, and workers. Some consider it the best way to eliminate the need for any outside childcare without the financial and career sacrifices of having one parent stay at home. Many find that ESP fits well with a simple life. A number of couples gravitate toward this lifestyle because they highly value family togetherness. Some men or women come to equal sharing from previously unsatisfying relationships built on traditional gender roles, seeking to do things differently this time around. Others have seen their own parents unhappy in traditional marriages. Some have previously decided, or suspected, that they didn't want children—only to find that parenthood finally fit them when they forged an equal and balanced relationship with a willing partner. Lesbian and gay parents are well represented in the ranks of ESP; they have had to build their own roles, without social gender rules to guide them, and often come up with model egalitarian relationships as a result. Some ESP couples are those who have married late, establishing themselves as experts in their work field and holding out for a mate who would be energized by an equal partnership. Many are young parents still in graduate school who are determined to share everything even at the expense of power careers they may never launch.

And then there's Marci and David. We've chosen to highlight their lives as an introduction to ESP not because they are a Hollywood rags-to-riches story or because they have achieved some flashy tabloid headline accomplishment. No massive change of heart caused either of them to quit a CEO position at a Fortune 500 company in favor of flipping burgers at a local restaurant. On the contrary, they are quietly living out happy lives with just a few tweaks to the path of the standard family. They value togetherness and sharing over amassing worldly wealth or high-level careers, and have carefully and purposefully structured their relationship to reflect these principles. If you could hang out with them, you'd notice that they don't spend much time arguing about who does what or seething about any unfairness in their relationship. Instead, they talk together about everything, and their connectedness is palpable. Like all of us, they are ordinary humans who have tough days, too. But they can't wait to sing each other's praises as a good parent and partner, and are dedicated to creating the best life for each other. Marci and David are, in many ways, a typical ESP couple.

Equality

HALVING IT ALL

"Equality" is such a loaded word. Who would be against equality and actually admit it? Yet when it comes to the lives of two parents, a whole world of polite individuals dismisses it on a daily basis. Why does one parent (not necessarily the same one) in almost every couple have more say over how the kids are raised, how the home is run, or whose career takes precedence? Why, after years of feminist marches, rallies, speeches, and writing, is the division of labor still unequal in so many homes and marriages? It is true that in general the battle cry for equality tends to come from women, but the stubborn imbalance is unfair to both women *and* men.

We believe that our society's continuing struggle to achieve full equality lies in its failure to drill this principle down into the details of our lives, and in forgetting about the advantages of equality for men. Decades have been spent inching the sexes forward toward equal voting rights, equal pay, and equal opportunity on the job or in the community. This is the work of creating

A WORD FROM AMY

Of ESP's two foundations, equality is the one that resonates most deeply with me. This has a lot to do with my childhood, which started innocently enough in a standard father-with-career/mother-stays-home family. But when I was eight, everything changed after my father took his own life. He was a brilliant man—a full professor of biochemistry at a major university before the age of forty and a pioneer in purine research—but he could not destroy the forces of his own troubled childhood and of severe depression.

This tragedy completely reshaped my life, but in one positive way it gave me the gift of a clean slate; it erased almost all imprinting of a traditional home from my memory, replacing it with a mom-does-it-all model and a lesson that women can be everything. My mother, who had left her own chemistry career when I was born, took a job teaching preschool so that she could pay the bills and still be home to care for me and my younger sister and maintain our household. Once we were a bit older, she returned to college for a start-from-scratch career in her true passion—graphic arts.

This history left me with a soul-deep wish that I not have to weather all of the family burdens alone when I became a mother, yet a fierce determination to be able to provide for my family at all times. My own mother did not remarry, and I did not get to experience again (for better or worse) having a father. But I took her strength with me into the world, and into my search for a partner—someone with whom to share equally in earning our way and raising a family.

external equality, and it is vital. But each of these advances is women-centric and is usually discussed in terms of benefits to a population rather than daily emotional or practical benefits to individuals. The real crime scene is now at the level of our marriages and families. The question to ask is not so much "Have we reached equality between men and women?" but "How equal is *my* relationship?" or "What would equality bring to each of *our* lives?"

What Is ESP Equality?

It's true that our culture often rewards breadwinners with more prestige and "value" than homemakers, and our economic structure supports this value system. But these concerns aside, we might envision that a traditional couple can still create an equitable relationship if both partners have jointly agreed to this arrangement and maintain full respect for each other's roles. He may earn all or most of the family paycheck; she may take on all or most of the daily childcare tasks and housework. But they are both devoted to the success of their family through their own largely separate-but-equal roles. Traditional couples can certainly be examples of equality as defined by the comparative value of two human beings and their contributions to the family.

However, equality doesn't have to stop here. If we can push it down deeper into our relationships, we can reach the kind of partnership that is more evenly shared on a day-to-day basis, in which both parents contribute equally to all that is needed to run a family—from tending a career to caring for their children. By leveraging the concept that two parents are fully capable in all family roles, we can arrive at the kind of equality that creates equally shared parenting. ESP equality hinges on the belief that both parents deserve to *be* full partners, and to *have* a full partner, in each of the four domains of childraising, breadwinning, housework, and time for self.

Like most new parents, Michelle and Jim from Bend, Oregon, started their parenting life in a traditional mold because, Jim explains, "We both just thought we were supposed to do it that way." Michelle quit her job teaching communications at a community college, and Jim took over a parking-lot-maintenance business, as they welcomed three baby girls into their family over the next four years. But underneath their seemingly standard-issue arrangement, this couple had a different dream waiting to emerge.

Michelle grew restless and resentful of Jim's working life, and Jim felt he was missing out on time with his girls. So they hatched a plan to break away from the pack. Michelle went back to school and then started her own communications consulting business, and Jim slowly scaled back his work to part-time, as the business allowed; they both ended up working about thirty hours per week. Simultaneously, they mapped out a weekly schedule that allowed each of them, on average, to handle half of the housework and childcare responsibilities.

It took considerable effort and time for Michelle and Jim to turn their relationship from one based on traditional gender roles to one based on full ESP equality. But both were motivated by the freedom that equal sharing brought to their relationship—a freedom from traditional roles and to experience the bounty of life. Michelle describes this motivation: "We both *want* to share caring for our girls equally and we *want* to share domestic duties and we *want* to do meaningful, engaging work outside of the home. Our life is now rich beyond measure compared to our early days of parenting. We share a deep understanding of the joy and struggle of caring for our babies as well as a mutual understanding of the challenges and satisfaction of work."

Over in Mountainview, California, software engineers Tom and Shankari took a slightly different path to their equal partnership. Shankari, like Michelle, took on primary parenting duties when their first daughter was born—but she figured out in only six weeks that staying at home left her feeling isolated and disconnected from the work she loved. Tom didn't want to "miss out on seeing my kids grow and change" but also did not feel it was wise to forfeit his career to stay home. Several less-than-satisfactory childcare arrangements had left this couple with a strong desire to minimize outside care, yet both had jobs that demanded full-time work. What to do?

Tom and Shankari's solution involved sequentially taking the maximum allowable parental leaves (twelve weeks) offered by their employers and then negotiating flexible work arrangements that optimized their efficiency on the job and their time with their daughter. Tom began commuting to his office most mornings and caring for their baby most afternoons, and Shankari scheduled the reverse shift with her employer. Both worked from home in the evenings and tag-teamed at least one day on the weekend to complete their work hours. Today, they have a second baby girl and are grateful for employers that place value on "making our deliverables" rather than on face time in the office. To make their lives less hectic, they have also made a conscious decision at this stage in their parenting lives to rely on outside help for much of their housework and to handle the physical care of Tom's disabled mother, who lives with them.

We have met and spoken with many couples like Jim and Michelle, and Tom and Shankari, who embody what is possible as a result of ESP's equality foundation. They don't live perfect existences, of course (and this is the case for all the couples described in this book—ourselves included!), but they are purposeful peers. The common thread in their stories is a desire for full partnership in the nitty-gritty of life. They accomplish this by each spending approximately equal *time* and having similar *investment* in each domain of their lives. The result offers three primary advantages that tend to build on each other: Each partner has to do only *half the work*, owns only *half the responsibility* for running the family, and gets *half the power* in the relationship.

Let's walk through each of these advantages in more detail.

Half the Work

On the surface, ESP equality resembles gender equality—at least in heterosexual relationships. No more will women be saddled with the bulk of the dishwashing, floor scrubbing, vacuuming, and meal prep! Finally, men will be required to do their fair share of diaper changing, rocking at 2:00 a.m., making school lunches, and playing Candy Land ad nauseam. Surely a feminist's dream. This perspective explains why many women ask where they can sign up . . . their husbands.

Not so fast.

There is little in the above scenario that could even remotely appeal to men. Why would *anyone* want to sign up for more work? Most men aren't lazy. They are working hard as well, even though their focus is classically on maintaining a career. They often leave home early, work late, sacrifice time with the kids, and live in a state of stress about money, deadlines, bosses, layoffs, retirement, bills, and so on. And now they are being asked to do more, without any clear payoff?

Let's face it. Lasting equality is going to take courage and a true interest by both parents. The challenge to most men will indeed be to embrace an increase in work at home and with the kids, but the corresponding challenge to women will be to hold on to equally meaningful careers, share the financial burden, and sacrifice time with the children and control over the home. When *all* the work of maintaining a home and family is recognized, acknowledged, and equally shared—and no one is *forced* to do anything—we're getting closer to ESP equality.

Many ESP couples say that dividing all the work is relatively easy once a mutual desire for equality is clear. We know this sounds crazy given that the division of chores can be one of the more contentious issues in a marriage. However, claiming the shared dream of equality is likely to create a sort of magic. Does a student who dreams of becoming a doctor begrudge having to study anatomy? Does a would-be NFL player need to be pushed to do his daily run or sit-ups? To these dreamers, necessary unpleasantries aren't a burden—they are a part of their journeys. With ESP, whether you're a man or a woman, a neat freak, or a slob, it is no longer just a chore to do your fair share of the dishes. Getting out there to earn your paycheck and taking your turn with the bedtime routines are simply things you expect to do for the privilege of ESP equality. Doing them makes you feel great about your place in the family and in your relationship.

Fair work division for ESP couples is simply the result of a wish to be happy together, as Michelle and Jim's story illustrates. This couple realized that they wanted something more from their lives as parents. Each understood that one of them was missing out on just what the other already had plenty of—for Jim, he had the satisfaction of a career and daily outside work, and for Michelle, she had time with their three sweet daughters. "Our goal now is to build our careers so that we can contribute equally from a time and energy perspective, allowing us equal and maximal time with the girls and as much time together as a family as possible," says Michelle. "We are both committed to each other's experience of a full and maximized life." Halving the *duties* of housework came easily to them once they recognized that they wanted to share the *joy* of parenting and having a career.

For Shankari and Tom, who have chosen to outsource much of their daily housework in order to prioritize work and time with their children, sharing the workload meant flexing their hours to match those most important to the culture at each of their jobs while stepping up to own their part of the childcare. "Once we realized we wanted to raise our daughter ourselves, I found I really liked it," said Tom of his solo-parenting time. "The conversation I had with my boss was a deal-breaker request for the schedule I needed to do my share."

With ESP, all of the work is shared—providing mental and physical relief for both partners and a joint appreciation of what it takes to keep the paychecks coming in, the house humming, and the kids fed. There is mutual admiration for time spent preparing a business proposal, folding laundry, dealing with problems at work, cleaning bathtub drains, sealing the new patio deck, or cleaning up after the almost-potty-trained. Both of you have a partner-in-crime to help solve problems and weather tough times. Neither of you shoulders all (or most) of the day-in, day-out monotony and isolation of work or home life. No one is stuck with all of *any* task. Neither of you has to say yes to every business trip or late-night meeting for fear that you'll miss a promotion on which your family's finances dangle. ESP can also provide an escape hatch for either of you should any specific aspect of life—a

BREAK OUT THE SPREADSHEETS?

One of the biggest misconceptions about ESP is the idea that it involves a perfect 50-50 split of every task and that if this is so, it leads to onerous charting to reach an even division of socks washed, kids tucked in bed, or overtime hours worked each week. As someone once wrote to us, "I don't want to live a kindergarten life where everyone needs the same color and number of crayons." Agreed!

Sharing the work of running a family is not about exact division by chore. The name for this lifestyle is not equally divided parenting but equally shared parenting; the point is not to put a hatchet into the middle of every activity. It is perfectly acceptable for one of you to do most of the lawn mowing and the other to handle most of the birthday party planning. Division by convenience, interest, or special expertise just makes sense!

It's true that with ESP you will want to share together to some degree in almost all of the tasks required to run your home and raise your children if you plan to reap the benefits of truly walking in each other's shoes. And you'll want the overall division of labor in each domain to be about equal between you. Discussing chore division and periodically mixing up the duties are energizing and positive because you want your division of labor to work—to be a source of fulfillment for both of you. But you and your partner are free to choose your own favorite "crayons" within each domain and celebrate that diversity.

terrible job, a difficult stage with the kids, a huge renovation project at home—prove intolerable. Your partner can hold down the fort while you get the breather you need or make adjustments to get out of the untenable situation. With shared work, you have your own built-in job share for the whole of your life.

Half the Responsibility

In many non-ESP families, even when a couple splits the cooking and shares in taking Johnny to soccer practice on the weekends, one parent is still often considered more capable at, or more responsible for, running the home and tending to the kids. And even when both parents work equal hours, it is typically one parent who invests more in a career and the other who supplements the family income with a more casual job. The responsibilities are still unequal, and this lopsidedness serves to keep couples focused on, or fighting about, task division. But when ESP equality is the goal, responsibility is fully shared instead. Claiming half the responsibility is foremost about a commitment by both partners to full *competence*. We can take a peek again into Jim and Michelle's home to get an appreciation of this notion.

Jim was no slouch around the house even when he worked full-time, and he'd even had a decent amount of experience taking the girls by himself for stretches at a time, but Michelle had been handling the bulk of the home responsibilities with gusto for four years. When Jim first began to take on half of the housework and childcare, he could have chosen to stay second fiddle—gritting his way through temper tantrums or fevers and cutting corners on meal preparation or cleanup on his watch—biding his time each day until Michelle returned to take over. But he had no interest in this halfhearted approach. "It was very important to me to be seen and felt as an equal by our girls," he says. "It was pretty tough, but to me there really didn't seem to be any choice but to plow through and establish myself with them." So he chose to take full responsibility—he would be every bit as good as Michelle! And Michelle backed away from holding on to her expertise to make room for Jim. When it came to comforting their children, Michelle explains, "I think part of the reason ESP worked relatively quickly for us is that those times when the girls asked for Daddy, I said 'fine' (usually out of relief, frankly, as I was exhausted from being the preference for so long), but he did not give in when they asked for me. He stuck it out and showed them that he could handle whatever was going on just as well. And he does."

Michelle in turn needed to take on responsibility for building her career—not as a hobby but as an equally legitimate means of providing the family's income. Jim was available to advise Michelle when she asked for input about starting her business, but he generally allowed her to grow and learn the necessary skills on her own, and supported her by believing in her dream and showing her that he was her equal partner. "Michelle has found something that really, *really* gets her driven career-wise, and she's strongly engaged in making it go," says Jim. "I'm so glad she's got something that she's excited about, and something that we both believe will be successful long term. I want her to have the time and the confidence in me to work on that comfortably." And while their actions were borne from a joint desire for equality, their growing all-around competence was infectious. The more they got good at things, the better they felt about their lives.

ESP equality breeds a joint pride in each domain. Once you have internalized a desire for equal partnership in your relationship, both of you care in detail about how the home is run and own the responsibility for making it a happy place to be. Both of you are committed to learning how best to care for your children and put that plan into action. You are equally invested in your careers, and can be assured that the other has no intentions of bowing out of paid work just to escape the frustrations or politics. We think this leads to an authentic life because no one is hiding behind fake excuses to avoid the real work of caring for your family, yourself, and each other.

In addition, competence works to eliminate those unpleasant behavior traits of nagging, criticizing, and bad-mouthing. Questioning or bringing something up for constructive discussion is encouraged, but negativity that transfers mental ownership back to one partner in any domain is counterproductive to equality. As an ESP partner, you are demonstrably capable of any task (or of asking for help if you're not) all by yourself. Your partner knows this, too. An ongoing commitment to cultivate an equal partnership helps parents treat each other like responsible adults.

Half the Power

Ah, the final frontier of marital equality! It is the equal sharing of power that represents the full depth of the ESP commitment to equal partnership. When two parents each claim half the power in the family, they *both* become powerful—as individual authorities and fully important leaders.

Pseudoequality is our word for a seemingly equal division of tasks and responsibility within a marriage but a still-unequal division of power. Both parents are pitching in and both are competent and grateful for each other's contributions, but something is

THE EFFICIENCY FACTOR

Some detractors of ESP have bemoaned the equal sharing of responsibilities as highly inefficient. Isn't it a duplication of efforts for two parents to take on the responsibility for running the house—both devoting time and energy to learning the contents of the freezer, the bedtime routines, and the kids' schedules? Wouldn't it make sense to hand all the cooking responsibilities to the parent who is a fantastic chef and spare the one who struggles not to burn the toast? We agree that asking each parent to become "good enough" at all aspects of the family's life has a learning-curve inefficiency that is circumvented in a traditional household.

But while we've already clarified that exact 50-50 division of any particular task is not a goal of ESP, neither is a 100-0 ratio. ESP means that you choose a team approach rather than let either parent become the sole specialist in large swaths of the childcare, housework, or breadwinning duties, even though a specific task may be done more often by the parent who has shown the most interest or aptitude for it. While there may be some initial start-up costs in making sure the home is run by two equally competent adults, the end result often makes up for any initial inefficiency. You each have complete freedom to leave your partner in charge without any need for advanced planning. Both of you can see the big picture rather than just your own carved-out family role. Both of you see and fully appreciate all the tasks that need to be done. Dinner may be duck à l'orange with truffle risotto on Tuesday and boxed macaroni and cheese on Wednesday, but neither of you is saddled with always—or never—cooking. And all members of the family will, by God, get the necessary nutrition. We say equality trumps short-term efficiency any day!

still amiss. "My husband helps out a lot at home—he does everything I ask him to do!" and "Sure, honey, you can buy a new couch" sound nice, but they smack of one parent owning the real authority. With pseudoequality, as with most traditional family arrangements, someone is always at the mercy of the other's edge in decision making.

When Jim and Michelle made a commitment to equality, they purposefully decided that neither of them would be subordinate to the other in any domain. Jim would not be a "junior" parent to Michelle—he would not be expected to take direction from her on what to feed the kids, how to dress them, or whether they'd be signed up for soccer or ballet. Nor would he be an apprentice homemaker assigned chores by Michelle and told how to do them. And while Jim made more money than Michelle, who was just beginning to court clients for her own consulting business, he would not have more say over how the family spent money. ESP equality eliminates any authority differential between two partners, so that all important decisions must be arrived at together, which fosters mutual cooperation rather than a ramrod approach to parenting, breadwinning, or homemaking "my way."

Shankari and Tom created an equal parenting life in the early stages, but demonstrate that equal power extends beyond how they make childcare, job, or homemaking decisions. With Tom's mother requiring constant care in their home, they carefully watch the power balance so that her presence does not become Shankari's primary duty. In fact, Tom maintains primary responsibility for his mother's care by purposeful decision. They have also agreed that the couple will live in the United States while Tom's mother requires their care. When this no longer becomes necessary, their plan is to move to Shankari's native India to be closer to *her* family.

With ESP, you are both equally important as individuals. Neither is stuck with the "less than" career—the one that is always the first to be compromised when the preschool calls to report that your child has a fever, or the one that is automatically cast aside if your honey wants to apply for a terrific job across the country. Neither of you gets first dibs by default on free time for personal hobbies. One spouse's wishes do not always dictate where the family will live. It is not more important for Mom to go to the parent-teacher conference if only one of you can attend. And Dad doesn't get to claim more of the fun playtime with the kids, saddling Mom with overseeing their homework and making sure they brush their teeth.

ESP power sharing is about seeing your partner as your equal

THE SAMENESS MYTH

But doesn't equal power overlook the uniqueness of two genders or two individuals? Isn't the family then left without a manager, rudderless in a sea of confusion? It can seem that way at first glance, but ESP is more like a family in which each domain is run by a two-person board of directors rather than a single dictator. Like the members of a board, ESP parents are their own people—not clones of each other.

This collaborative approach opens the door to learning from each other. "I've learned to say yes to my kids' crazy ideas more often, rather than my knee-jerk no—by watching my wife with them," says one ESP dad. His wife responds with how her husband has "taught me how to be present and energized with them, rather than always multitasking and splitting my attention in five different directions." It is equal power, which garners equal respect, that makes this learning possible in ESP relationships—time and again. Each parent's strengths can buoy the other's weaknesses, so that both have a chance at becoming the best worker, parent, homemaker, and person in the end. This is true because ESP parents have each other's backs—they are not adversaries attempting to usurp each other but partners dedicated to leading and learning together.

and stepping out of the way to allow him or her to take charge as often as you do. But ESP couples also say they are ceding the real power to the team of two rather than anointing one parent as king or queen of anything. While ESP couples sometimes clash over how to handle decisions just like any other couple, they have eliminated the underlying power imbalance and harnessed the power of two open minds to come up with the best solutions.

The Equality Foundation

While it is women who may initially flock to the idea of equality as a way to have their partners step up to half the work of child-raising and housework, it is men who often bring it to full reality for a couple. Men who don't hide from all it takes to run a home and care for their children. Men who want equal say at home and shared responsibilities for bringing home the bacon. Men who covet an intimate relationship with their kids and have no need to be their wives' apprentices in this relationship. Both men and women benefit from choosing equality as a core element of their relationship—equally.

Regardless of which partner initiates the discussion to create ESP, the key to its ultimate goal—the happiness of both parents—is that both of you are fully on board for the ride. We encourage you to talk together about what it means to be truly equal partners, in the ESP definition of equality, and decide together if this is your idea of a great life. Just like that athlete training for NFL stardom, the medical student memorizing her anatomy notes, the ESP mother who goes to her job as often as her husband, or the ESP father who willingly and joyfully washes his share of dishes, you will both need to keep the prize of equality in mind as you work your way over its hurdles.

Temptations to exert control over your spouse in a domain will be strong and understandable. Our culture is full of covert and overt claims that women are more capable parents and homemakers, or that being manly means having a powerful career and making more money than your wife. Don't be surprised if you catch yourself, or your partner catches you, in a blatant act of inequality from time to time ("You're feeding him wrong!" "You can quit your job when I get my promotion!" "My child is not going to wear that!"). In a traditional relationship, the idea that your way is superior might be allowed due to the overwhelming time advantage that each of you has in a particular domain. But in an ESP relationship, this is no longer a wise assumption; both of you are capable and willing participants in all aspects of your lives, and you choose to work out your differences as equal partners instead.

Communication can also be a hurdle to ESP equality. Or as one ESP mom told us, "This is hard work! Instead of just complaining that my husband isn't available, I have to confront all the issues with him directly." Although we will explore the details of communication as it relates to each domain in future chapters, it is important to note here that ESP is not a good plan of action for two parents who don't enjoy working things out together. It requires love, respect, and a willingness to engage in all the conversations—however enlightening or difficult they might be—that happen in ESP homes. We love that no stone gets left unturned with these discussions, that no topic is off-limits, and that they happen in the spirit of exploration rather than accusation. "How can we figure out together what is best?" an ESP couple might ask. But still, the asking must occur.

To get past these barriers, and others we'll explore later in discussing each domain, ESP couples focus on the big picture. They consciously choose equality as a foundation for their relationship, along with embracing the foundation of balance discussed in the next chapter, because they feel it offers the possibility of their best life together. As one ESP father states, "To me, every real relationship is based in equality, and raising a family with my partner is just a natural extension of this philosophy." Equal time and investment in each domain is the goal for ESP equality, not as a mission for equality's sake alone, nor as a quest for perfection, but as part of the very definition of a relationship between two partners.

The Real Comparison

As a generation, we often pat ourselves on the back for demonstrating far more equality than that of our own parents. Women are in the workforce in record numbers. Men are doing more childcare and housework than ever before. "Hooray!" say statisticians and business leaders and sociologists. Well, how about a "that's nice" instead? We are calling on all parents to reach for something even more exciting—the kind of equality that matters to individual couples and that shapes their relationships to make both parents happy. We're suggesting that we compare each man's work, responsibility, and power only to those of his partner, not to those of his forebears, and that we compare each woman's contributions to the family only to those of her husband.

This challenge is not meant to shame any of us, as we don't believe that separate but equal is a shameful position. But in our own lives, and in the lives of the ESP couples we know, the comparison is necessary. Equality in its full sense gives us authenticity—to live every day knowing we are doing our fair share of the work, we are responsible for the results, and we have the power to make it all happen. It can also lead us to extraordinary intimacy with our partners—as full equals in each domain. We want the best for each other, far beyond the tedious he said/she said of equal task division, and we get the best in return.

Balance

HAVING IT ALL

A balanced life is often ridiculed as impossible—a goal that many have abandoned because it makes us mere mortals feel bad when we can't achieve it. We generally strive just to make it through each day, especially if we are the parents of young children. Attempting to also gracefully balance it all, scratching out optimum fulfillment in the process, seems like an extremely tall order! Like equality, balance is a cultural ideal that appears beyond our grasp. Should we simply give up and give in to the chaos?

Or maybe we're just not trying hard enough. So say the cheery headlines on feel-good magazines in the grocery store checkout line that promise the secrets to balancing it all. They tease us by intimating that they know our pain and that we're just one step away from eliminating it forever. Just another slight nudge and—voilà!—stress-free living will snap into place. If we would only take up the habit of breathing deeply for five minutes every morning and evening, our lives would be more at peace. If we bought that new super-lightweight stroller, or got a Black-Berry, or ditched our BlackBerry, or stopped making the bed, or scheduled pretend appointments to steal time for ourselves—then we could be calm and happy. A little quick fix—that's all we need! But deep down, we all know the truth: this stuff doesn't really make much of a difference. Something bigger is at the core of our collective inability to feel balanced.

In this chapter, we invite you to look at balance in a new way—as a quality that arises from the overarching structure of your life rather than from implementing any perky tips to fix it. This view of balance is the second foundation of equally shared parenting and it's yours for the taking. If you think it's not possible, we suggest you follow Steve Martin's advice, when he opened his *Saturday Night Live* monologue in October 1973 by saying, "I like to start each day by doing something that is impossible." Let's get started ourselves. . . .

The Good Stuff

Going to work can be a lot of fun. Yes, there will be office politics, difficult people, tedious projects, and plenty of other frustrations. But pursuing a career allows you to connect with your place in the world as a worker—sometimes as a key contributor and some-times as a team player in the company's mission. It is a means to enjoy the fruits of your education and to interact with others in a significant way. It gives you a chance to put forth your best and

A MESSAGE FROM MARC

My quest for balance began long before I was married. As a young man, I took the standard route presented to American males—I applied my freshly earned mechanical engineering degree to long hours and hard work as I climbed up the ranks at a large company. I also attended business school full-time in the evenings and relied on adrenaline, coffee, and dreams of future career success to sustain me. But there was a persistent flaw in my plan—one I discovered by playing a game of asking myself what I wanted to do "next Tuesday." My little amusement turned into a challenge I couldn't ignore. No matter how much I enjoyed my job (and I did) or enjoyed going to school (and I did), when Tuesday came, I usually wished for something other than work to occupy my day.

I toyed with the idea of looking for a new job; maybe a new location, a big adventure, or more pay could hold my interest and inspire me to make peace with my nagging question. As luck would have it, I got the opportunity to face this option head on. A senior business colleague was planning on retiring in the next few years and asked me to take over his engineering company. He had thirty-five full-time employees and a world of challenge to keep me occupied. After a few meetings to explore the transition, however, I surprised him by backing out. I had a different plan for my life. The plan was not formulated yet, but I knew it wasn't going to include decades of Tuesdays in which I wanted to be somewhere else.

For the next few years, I paid down my debt and simplified my life as I fumbled my way toward a new lifestyle. I tinkered with the standard masculine prescriptive by asking for a schedule change (first rejected, then approved on a temporary basis) in which I worked three 8-hour days a week for six months. I attribute this experiment to solidifying my commitment to enjoy work on a more regular basis—by fitting it to my life rather than the reverse. When Tuesday came around, I was energized, clearheaded, and eager to plow through my workload. What began as a game ended with the discovery of, and a dedication to, living a balanced life.

see the consequences, invent new and better ways of doing things, or learn something new every day. And you might even get to devote a large chunk of your life to a purpose you genuinely value. The workplace can provide plenty of worth. Why not grab as much as you can?

What about being home with the kids? We all know this is not always fun and games; as a parent, thousands of moments try your patience. But there are pinnacle times, too: When you take happy, healthy, obedient kids on a beach day adventure, or sail through the dinner and homework routine with laughter all around; that lovely feeling of catching your infant's first smiles, of watching your baby taste ice cream, of giving one of your kids a much-needed hug after a tough day. But truly enjoying family time hinges on so much more than these brief moments. It comes from being a part of the wonder—watching them grow and learn, catching their untainted enthusiasm, helping them understand the ways of the world, loving them so that they can confidently take risks. Being available and open to this possibility, in all its messiness, is a privilege. Why miss a moment of this adventure?

Then there's housework. Most of us don't cherish scrubbing the toilets or endlessly folding laundry. Sure, sometimes cleaning or cooking can make you feel terrific about staying on top of your game, or garner compliments from your partner or the kids. But housework is mostly just something that all of us try to fit into an already crowded day. Would things be different if you had lots of extra time to polish and organize? Some of us truly enjoy paying the bills, washing the car, vacuuming (really, Amy loves it), or building and fixing things (that's Marc). Cooking is a meditative pleasure for many. Whatever your fancy, there is something about connectedness to where you live that is fundamental to the human experience. Your home is the place you come to after being out "there"; it is your haven and a reflection of your interests and style. Taking the time to care for it—be that getting your hands dirty in the garden or placing the clean laundry in the drawers of those you love—keeps you rooted to the wholeness of your life. Even if time crunches may lead you to outsource some activities to housecleaners or carpenters, the time you do spend caring for your surroundings is literally grounding. It's not that bad after all.

And don't forget about time for yourself. There's a world of entertainment, hobbies, social activities, exercise, and community service—or just a good night's sleep—to be enjoyed! So many of us maintain that we don't have enough time to take care of ourselves or seek out adventure and smell those roses. How nice it would be if we all had plenty of time to fritter away doing what we pleased.

Putting It All Together

It is clear that there's plenty of satisfaction and enjoyment to be had in life, whether you are at work, home, or play. That's not exactly a news flash. A stay-at-home parent hones in on the joy that comes from the kids and home, a sole breadwinner gets fulfillment primarily from work, and a typical dual-income couple attempts to squeeze in enough of both worlds. We're not going to rate these choices in order of importance. But we'll point out what most traditional couples already acutely know: their choices include important sacrifices. Staying at home means letting go of what outside work brings to your life; focusing primarily on work doesn't make room for the intimacy of full-on childraising and connection with your home; and juggling it all can mean little time for self-rejuvenation. By letting go of any of the four life domains, these standard-option partners are each leaving a lot of joy on the table.

In contrast, ESP partners build their lives so that they share responsibilities across *all* domains—leading to different sacrifices than those of traditional parents. Instead of making your work the centerpiece of your life, ESP asks a main breadwinner to scale back to a more flexible career or even to part-time employment to make room for a partner's equally valuable career. Neither you nor your partner takes full credit for keeping a tidy home, settling instead for the shared work of "good enough." And both of you give up some, but neither gives up *all*, of the time you previously enjoyed to yourselves before parenthood. If you're a father, you let go of our culture's claim that yours is the more essential career. If you're a mother, you make another sacrifice of sorts—you invite your children's father to share in your societal prerogative to be the primary parent.

The sacrifices of ESP, however, have a powerful upside in allowing both of you to have a balanced life. Instead of splitting up the joys, you choose to give each other a decent dose of all of them. You stay in the working world without allowing your career to overtake your life, and can still contribute meaningfully in a job you love. But you make room to expand that love to include a substantial amount of guaranteed time alone with your children. With two parents working flexible or reduced schedules, your children's daycare needs are more than would be required if one of you stayed home but less than if you both worked standard full-time schedules. Neither of you is stuck doing most of the housework.

And in most cases, you both still have ample time for yourselves and each other.

ESP parents strive for a meaningful capacity to experience the wonder, joy, connection, challenge, and stimulation of all four domains of life at once. They also recognize and respond to the truth that time is irretrievable. Kids grow up and can't be put in a box on the shelf until we've got the time to bond with them; adventures or career opportunities present themselves once and expire if not taken; chances to visit family or connect with close friends (or with each other as a couple) come up and are gone again. So they opt for real-time balance—in the right personal mix for each of them.

The Truth About Balance

True balance, in the ESP sense, is a means of prioritizing your time in the four domains of work, children, home, and self so that you can honestly say "I wouldn't want to be anywhere else" at any given time—even if you are up to your elbows in a tedious project at work, wrestling with a baby who won't nap, or sorting mountains of dirty laundry. Of course, you won't instantly relish every chore, responsibility, or situation. No need to train yourself to like washing dishes more than going to the movies! Your declaration reflects less about loving every moment *itself* and more about loving your whole life at any moment and being at peace with the way you structure your time.

Equally sharing the load in each domain allows for this type of thinking because neither parent spends *too much time* doing any one thing. With your time and energy balanced between all domains, you have a greater chance of staying in the moment wherever you are than if you got stuck in one area at the expense of others. Neither of you ends up unhappily overworking or doing all the carpooling or chores in a life that grinds on and on.

"After three or four days at home or at work, I'm ready for the next thing," says ESP dad Dave, a nephrologist who works a 50 percent schedule and shares the care of his four children with his wife, Liz (also a part-time physician) in Pittsburgh, Pennsylvania. "I don't feel overworked or overburdened in any one area." Liz agrees, and adds, "Our schedules let us enjoy our home life *and* our career life—we have closer relationships with our kids and feel less burnout than almost any other doctor we know."

Many ESP couples work part-time, like Liz and Dave, as a means to attain balance most easily. But others find their own individual balance in full-time work. ESP parents who work full-time differ from the standard dual-income couple because they tend to connect their work lives directly to their core values; every day at work for each of them is a day spent doing what they want to project onto the world and into the minds of their children, and nourishes their souls. "Full-time work makes me happy," says Cynthia, a Boston, Massachusetts, ESP mom and elementary school principal. Her husband, Imari, who directs a nonprofit mentoring business, confirms this sentiment: "I wouldn't want to work less because my work matches who I am." Their three children often volunteer with them for community service work at Imari's company on weekends. "I want this life of service to be in my children's very skin," Imari tells us.

Each of us is granted only twenty-four hours in a day, to be filled as we see fit. ESP challenges you to fill them consciously, aware of the trade-offs you must make regardless of your decision, and to choose a healthy mix of what you hold most dear.

MEDIOCRITY

One might argue that a balanced life is a mediocre life. If you devote yourself to experiencing it all, you never get to fully master any one aspect. You are left knowing a little bit about a lot of things and doing none of them very well, right?

Life is full of pros and cons, sacrifices and benefits. If you choose to pour your time into researching theories of relativity, you may become the next Einstein (or not), but your decision will surely guarantee that you won't be America's next top chef. In this respect, we truly can't have it all—and ESP won't solve this problem. The balance afforded by ESP gives us well-rounded parenting lives and prevents either partner from sacrificing a fun life the moment a child is born.

Although the world needs individuals who are able to devote their lives to singular missions—to be our presidents and baseball hall-of-famers—their decisions do have consequences. The personal consequence is mediocre (or nonexistent) balance. The wider loss is the chance for their partners to be everyday equals. ESP awards you with a wonderful life—one in which you can experience many things in smaller doses, and be in a position to give enough to your job, to your children, in service to others, and to yourself. It gives the same opportunity to your partner. With a balanced life, we can have it all—just not in extreme doses. To us, that's anything but mediocrity.

A Bird in the Hand

"Time waits for no man"—or woman. "No one ever died wishing he'd spent more time at the office." "Life's short—eat dessert first." The clichéd phrases are endless, but the messages are so poignant because they clash with how we're expected to construct our lives. Our culture's dictum is more like "He who dies with the most toys wins." Put in your time at the office now; enjoy your life in the golden years. Stay home with the kids, and then when they are in elementary school (or maybe off to college), you can think about a career for yourself again. Or as some women's career advocates suggest, live without time for yourself for a couple of decades so that you don't miss a beat in your profession while you are mired in mothering young children. These attitudes say that someday balance will be possible, but only once one of life's four domains—such as a career or childraising—is simply no longer applicable. Today, however, you must buck up and get through life without it. On the flip side, we have the believers in external gratification as a payoff for hard work: enjoying life to the fullest includes "buying" into the belief that more will make you happy. You will need to earn even more money (or go into debt) so that you can book premier vacations, own the best car or live in the best neighborhood, send your children to the best private college, or even buy the latest time-saving gadget.

An ESP life doesn't allow us to subscribe to either the enjoy-life-later or the superficial-experience-at-a-price philosophy of balance. Each of these options requires a tremendous sacrifice that ESP couples are unwilling to make—waiting for joy or burdening themselves with the need for more cash.

Simi and her husband, Pete, are not yet retired in the classical sense. They were trained as software engineers in their native Canada and worked long hours in their younger days. But about ten years ago, Pete convinced Simi to move to the natural beauty of the Colorado mountains and begin living their dreams. They continued to work hard but began to live simply and save rather than spend much of their earnings for the next few years. And then they quit their software jobs. Today, they get up together whenever it suits them, and each works about ten to fifteen hours per week—Pete as a carpenter and Simi as a financial manager who is primarily home-based. They enjoy month-plus-long vacations to visit family or to explore the world. They are, as Pete says, "checking off" their goals in life, such as learning the art of plumbing; the practice of real estate; or how to play the guitar, garden sustainably, or find time simply to read quietly.

In order to make ends meet, Simi and Pete spend little and budget carefully (we'll tell you more about their tactics in Chapter 8), but they can't think of a better way to spend their days. This existence is what many of us look forward to at retirement. If Pete and Simi were in their early sixties, this wouldn't be so unusual, right? But they are also the parents of a four-year-old son, and they are both only thirty-five years old.

A balanced life doesn't always involve such extraordinary changes. Melissa and Richard in Arlington, Massachusetts, illustrate a more moderate approach to balance in their shared desire to be home with their children. When their first child was born, Richard altered his job as a jazz pianist and director of a piano academy so that he clocked only twenty hours per week plus some evening gigs. Melissa, the director of quality assurance for a software company, also reduced her work hours—to about thirty per week. Together, they devised a schedule that eliminated any outside childcare and accommodated a second child. Both Melissa and Richard wanted their jobs to take a backseat to being with their children and being all together as a family, but neither wanted to stay at home exclusively. Their solution to the balance puzzle also allows them to share the housework evenly and make time for Richard's daily swim workout and Melissa's running routine.

Whether your definition of a balanced life looks like Simi and Pete's or more like Melissa and Richard's (or something still more standard), and whether you strive for minimal outside childcare or are content with any particular choice in a range of childcare options, there will always be financial considerations associated with creating this type of balance. This is why so many of the ESP couples we know identify with efforts to live simply and to purposefully step off the treadmill of materialism as a means of happiness. As we'll explore in more detail in Chapter 8, ESP balance is not achieved by squandering our futures but rather by creating a life of "enough" that is sustainable for the long haul. It is not about looking forward to complete retirement from paid work but rather structuring your life so that work can fit into a well-rounded life for decades to come. Or as ESP mom Liz says, "I could do this till I'm eighty years old!"

Permission to Play

All this balance might make some of us a little queasy. Isn't grown-up life supposed to be hard? Getting to the point where you can enjoy where you are goes against the standard way our culture operates. We expect drudgery, we're taught to work as much as we can to make as much money and get as far ahead as possible, and our culture even rewards us for taking on too much by allowing us to complain and sigh and act like martyrs. It is almost unimaginable that someone would turn down a raise or promotion even if it involves more work. It is decidedly uncool to feel that we are paid properly and have the appropriate amount of responsibility; we're taught to always want more of both. We're trained to think of ourselves as indispensably important yet not quite entitled to a balanced life.

When was the last time someone told you he wasn't "busy"? On the contrary, it is downright un-American to be understressed and unbusy. Similarly, we're all conditioned to live for next weekend or our next vacation because, God knows, our regular lives are so terrible! Almost everyone loves vacations, of course. But what if you could simply look forward to the next one with the mind-set of "I'm so excited to be going to Paradise Island" rather than "I need this trip to Paradise Island *so* much"? With ESP balance, a vacation is a chance to try something different or see friends or family or see the world, but it is not a reset button. You've carefully built your life so that you can enjoy it day in and day out without *needing* a vacation.

Marco and Megan live in Petaluma, California, and care together for their three young children. Megan enjoys a flexible full-time position as an IT security consultant, and Marco works two-thirds' time as a high school English and history teacher. When we asked Marco about his decision to scale back at work, he explained that this was not his first foray into trading money for balance. To become a high school teacher, he had already resigned himself to a lower salary than he could have commanded, and now he accepts even lower wages. But it was all worthwhile because he could escape what he calls the "trap of a money-oriented job that prevents people from enjoying life." Marco hears friends and acquaintances complain about their weary lives all the time, and this grates on him. "Most white-collar workers take it for granted that they will hate their jobs," he says. "I love my job!"

There is nothing noble about being too busy, tired, and depleted to enjoy life. ESP requires dispensing with someone else's version of your life and claiming your own version instead—whether that is through part-time or flexible full-time work. Foremost, it gives you permission to stand up for your own right to a balanced life—and to recognize the beauty of the same for your partner.

SCOREKEEPING

The antithesis to sharing balanced lives is probably "every man for himself." Yet this is what some have mistaken for the reality of equally shared parenting. The idea here being that ESP requires, or leads to, scorekeeping and accounting and he says/she says arguing about how many minutes each parent has spent washing the dishes this week, as if ESP referred to some kind of point system. How unpleasant, and unloving, this idea seems—and how foreign to the very core of this lifestyle.

There is a world of difference between keeping tabs on what your spouse does around the house and having a system to share the duties evenly so that both of you can have balanced and happy lives. There is no doubt that ESP requires you to think outside the norm, and to work together to figure out how the necessary chores will get done and how cultural inequalities won't seep into your relationship over time. Discussions between partners are crucial—both to set up your initial plan for equal sharing and to keep it real as circumstances change or substantial inequalities are suspected. But the daily focus is on doing your own share of the work and honoring your partner's ability to do the same. Let's leave scorekeeping to the sports teams.

The Balance Foundation

One thing that Portland, Oregon, ESP dad Brian loves about his life is all the time he gets with his preschool son, Declan. His in-laws recently offered to watch their grandson on Brian's normal Daddy Day, but Brian declined. "But I *like* my Fridays with Declan!" he explains. Now that he's got a good life going, Brian says the stakes are too high for him to ever return to a standard work schedule—to let work (or even loving grandparents) infringe on time with his son.

Why would Brian, or any parent, make a balanced life such a priority? For ESP couples, balance represents an enjoyable and meaningful life—the kind that can be had today and sustained into the future. By giving up what is expected, we are free to work out a unique solution that fills both of our lives with all that we value most from each domain. We're not torn between work and family—home and the big wide world. Seldom are we filled with guilt for being somewhere physically and somewhere else in spirit. "Our lives just give us time for *life*," says ESP mom Amy of Brookline, Massachusetts. "We have so much time to be together as a family."

This view of balance differs markedly from those magically balanced lives promised at the newsstand. Glossy pictures paint balance as unruffled poise and days that run like clockwork. Yet there is not a parent alive—practicing ESP or not—who does not have horror stories of crazy days or genuine crises. Balance naysayers tell us disorder and mess are just par for the course with kids and that we'd better make peace with chaos—accept that this is our lot for years to come and skip trying for anything better. Talk-show balance gurus say we can fix the problem by being more efficient. But as much as we love efficiency and acceptance, we say they've all got it wrong.

You can't eliminate uncertainty, but you can go one better than making peace with this craziness or buying some new gizmo to keep track of it all. You can *love* it. This is possible when you don't settle for it being your everyday norm. Real balance, as a core foundational principle of ESP, means setting priorities so that life with kids is not one overwhelming day after another any more than your work life is endless runs of twelve-hour days.

Philosophically, balance and equality are two separate ideas that make up the mind-set of equally shared parenting. But in a real

ESP partnership, these two foundations are so intertwined that they cannot be separated. Equality without balance doesn't exclude the possibility that both partners are equally miserable, and balance without equality ignores the need to tend your relationship together. We didn't know this when we met. Marc had paid no attention to the advantages of equality in pursuit of his individually balanced life, while Amy had searched for a peer above all other concerns. It was only when our wishes collided that we could see exactly how well they fit together.

Both foundations together ignite full-out ESP. By balancing your life, in concert with your equal partner's balanced life, you both get breaks from the occasional crazy days in any role. You share the load, the joys, and a full life in which—by your own definition—you each have it all.

PART
TWO

BUILDING THE STRUCTURE

t is time to turn from the question, "Why build a relationship on equality and balance?" and begin to dig into the how. Once you and your partner have reached a personal belief in equally shared parenting as your best life together, you are fully equipped to make it real. Of course, a few specifics would be helpful.

In the next four chapters, we will concentrate on building the structural components of ESP. These are the four domains that make up its everyday practice:

Children—sharing the joy, work, and responsibility of raising your kids

Career—sharing the breadwinning duties and the satisfaction of a meaningful career

Home—caring for your home as a team of equals

Self—maintaining enough personal time (and time together) to keep you both satisfied

Each domain is examined in a separate chapter, although of course in real life they all coalesce on a daily basis. Keep in mind that the overall goal is for both of you to have approximately equal time and investment in each—allowing a balanced life for both partners. Throughout the rest of the book, the reasons to reach for equal sharing in each domain continue to be equality and balance. It is with a shared commitment to these ideals that all the practicalities become doable— even easy.

Children

PRIDE AND JOY/GREATEST GIFT

We were almost two years into our experiment of sharing the hands-on care of our daughter when we found ourselves at a friend's home one afternoon. There were seven couples and close to ten kids gathered for a cookout. Marc was enjoying a beer on the deck and talking shop with a few of the other dads, while Amy was chatting with another mom in the yard close to the swing set.

Then it happened: Maia fell off the swing. The crash wasn't serious but scary enough that she launched into an all-out-crying search for comfort. She ran right past Amy, screaming, "Daddy, Daddy!" all the way across the yard into Marc's open arms. As we confirmed that Maia was unhurt and she returned to happy play,

Amy wondered briefly if the other moms had judged her for not being our daughter's automatic parent of choice. But later we agreed that the overwhelming thought for both of us was, *We did it.*

A Team of Two

A childraising partnership is a challenge, without a doubt. In almost every culture, mothers are expected to take the lead—even to the point of near exclusivity—in caring for children, and fathers are expected to let them. By necessity, then, the path to equalizing childraising involvement will require both parents to ignore these expectations. ESP childraising takes a redefining of caregiving, particularly of motherhood, as women let go of their grip on parenting, and men step in as full participants.

It is tempting to dive into dissecting these gender assignments right away, but we would like to take a moment first to address the basics of any couple's plan for sharing this immense, joyful, and often overwhelming domain. In order to succeed, both of you will need to be on the same page—to be clear about your *dedication to childraising as a team of equals.* This attitude says, "We are in this together." It conveys a commitment to sharing the pleasure and pain of parenting, and figuring out how to tackle the mountains of diapers, the hours of play, and the subtleties of discipline. It acknowledges that you're in deep with the details on a daily basis, so that both of you can balance childraising with the whole of your lives.

Talking together in open conversation, and making a joint commitment to this team approach up front, allows both of you to face your own challenges as you put action to your words. So we highly recommend that you take time to understand each other's expectations and hopes for parenthood—motherhood and fatherhood.

With your plan out in the open, you are ready to turn to the individual work of equally shared childraising—the work that prepares each of you to put your team goal into practical action. The challenges here start by asking you to recognize the traditional roles played by each parent, then to reject those that are based solely on gender, and finally to replace those stereotypes with your own definitions. We'll split our discussion, then, into what is expected of *mothers* in order to share the care of children (narrated by Amy), followed by how *fathers* can reach equal childraising (narrated by Marc). After we address the work in store for each of you separately, we'll come back together for a discussion of how you can meld your individual efforts to accomplish the daily practicalities of equally sharing in raising your children.

Letting Go: Equal Childraising for Mothers

From the moment I first saw that little pink plus sign on my pregnancy test, I couldn't wait to get Marc involved. I plowed through books detailing each week of gestation, and then moved on to learning about babies themselves—through more books, websites, and talking with every mom I could find. This is how I approach any new and exciting project. But alas, it is decidedly *not* how Marc operates. In fact, the more I prodded, pushed, and begged him to read what I was devouring, or even to discuss the topic of babies, the more he said he didn't feel like participating "quite yet." He claimed he wanted to be my coparent, but already I couldn't get him to do anything! My anxiety started to build, and my fears of becoming the stereotypical fully responsible mother added fuel to my already hormonal state. But then it dawned on me: nobody wants to be controlled.

Nobody responds well to shame, guilt, ridicule, or any other trick I was trying on Marc in those early days. Yes, if we were to have a shot at doing this baby thing as equals, I was going to have to learn to let go. I had to allow Marc to be himself and trust that he would make good on his promise—in his own way. And I had to recognize that equal meant equal—not me directing him to do an equivalent amount of work *my* way. How easy it would have been for me to single-handedly screw up a good thing!

Now, after seven years of cultivating an equal partnership with Marc using a slightly different approach, I've had a chance to practice my skills of letting go, and I believe in its value more than ever. But I'm also left with an even deeper appreciation for the effort that is required. Other ESP moms tell me that they, too, do not belittle the work that goes into relinquishing primary-parent status. Through their stories and mine, I can distill this effort into three essential warnings to women. If you want lasting and happy equal childraising with your partner, you will need to:

1. Stop thinking of babies and children as your *territory*.
2. Quit taking on more than half the childraising *work and responsibility*.
3. Give up the *right* to be your child's most important parent.

Territory

How many men pick out their baby's diaper bag? How many dictate when their baby will be weaned from the pacifier? Not many, I would venture. Even if we solicit feedback from our spouses, it is usually mothers behind most decisions that involve children. Our territorial markings may show up as Mom's minivan, Mom's decision about cosleeping, Mom's feeding schedule, or Mom's choice of crib sheets. When we were pregnant, we were obviously in charge of everything related to growing a baby. But once our babies become separate family members, we must recognize the fallacy of continuing this practice if we want equal partners in raising our kids. We already know that ESP requires us to share overall decision-making power in order to achieve equality; sharing *territory* is the way this happens in the child-raising domain.

ESP began for Anna and Alex of Helsinki, Finland, the moment their first child was born. Alex stayed home for almost three months to do his share alongside Anna (Alex tells us a more typical paternity leave is a still-generous five weeks long for Finnish men). While Anna breastfed exclusively, Alex dug into fatherhood by doing almost everything else. Of particular satisfaction to him was a little notebook he kept on the ins and outs of diapering a baby. The couple had decided together to use cloth diapers, so Alex recorded which types of fabrics leaked and which didn't, and whether folding or securing them one way yielded better results than another way. He then recommended a brand and a method for the family. Anna agreed without question.

Involving a man so early in the babycare game is more common today than even several years ago. But this little example shows a couple who took the man's equal say in baby stuff literally and with pride. In order for their equality to work, Anna had to disown the cultural belief that baby stuff like a diaper brand decision was hers to choose and his to accept. She had to consciously fight against any autopilot moves that made her the primary parent and trust that Alex's way of gathering information and making decisions was as valid as hers. She could do this because she understood what most ESP couples know: the more entrenched a mother gets in babycare decisions on her own, the less likely her partner will feel a joint ownership. And the more she directs her partner, the more likely he'll end up being her dissatisfied servant rather than her equal. When her husband is free to select the diapers, Anna knows that he'll be fully invested in using them.

Sharing each step along the way allows your partner to stay fully involved—as an equal member of the two-parent team. The earlier you can accept the idea that he's equally entitled to weigh in on decisions, the easier it will be for equal childraising to come naturally later on. Here is some more advice for sharing the early childraising territory from other ESP moms:

- When you are pregnant, view your "birth plan" as the story of the birth of your family rather than just your own personal experience. Your husband becomes a father at the same moment that you become a mother. Decide *together* how this day should play out (yes, even though it is your body doing the birthing).

- Involve your husband in determining childcare routines/schedules (e.g., the nap schedule) so that they evolve jointly rather than as your sole creation.

- Don't assume that you get to pick out the stroller, decorate the nursery, or buy the children's clothes for next season. These, and any other preparations, can be given to either of you or tackled together.

- Be open to ways your husband can bond equally with the baby. Women have breastfeeding to create intimacy, but men can take the lead on baby wearing, for example.

- If you have any control over your baby shower guest list, ask that it be a coed event. If you plan to create a gift registry, do so together.

- If your husband asks you questions about how to care for the baby, ask him for *his* opinion rather than give him *your* answer. Your response to, "Honey, when are we going to start feeding her solids?" could be, "Hmmm . . . I've read different things. What do you think about waiting until six months?" rather than a definitive, "When she's six months."

- Take time to listen to parenting tips from your spouse, and try out his ideas.

Work and Responsibility

If we can stop ourselves from unilaterally making all the childcare decisions, it stands to reason that we can then also let go of doing all the work and taking full responsibility. Yet this is easier said than done! Unfortunately, our culture gives us a strong message that growing our babies into high-achieving, trustworthy, happy adults is our job—not our husbands'. Our partners may pack lunches, shop for birthday presents, handle baths and bedtime routines, and bandage boo-boos, but somehow we can still so easily think we're the ones with the ultimate responsibility.

We've all heard traditional moms complain that when they are sick, they're still expected to care for the kids; but when a father is sick, he typically gets to rest. But we know that ESP equality means not only sharing the power but also sharing the work and responsibility. It's time to shed the old way of thinking. The two myths we need to bust as ESP moms are that childcare duties belong to us because we're (1) *female* and because we're (2) *better* at them.

Many women are tripped up early on by the very real fact that only a female can *breastfeed*. Since breastfeeding can initially require many hours each day, it can serve to tip the babycare responsibilities and overall time devoted to childraising far in Mom's direction if a couple chooses to breastfeed. This can even lead to subsequent inequality if they are not proactive in holding on to their plans to share the work. But ESP parents sidestep this trap with a few common strategies:

- Make sure your baby is nursing well, and then introduce a bottle of pumped milk fed by Dad every day. Many couples designate this bottle as one of the middle-of-the-night feeds so that both partners are assured of a decent stretch of sleep every night during those first few crazy months.

- Choose a feeding schedule with relatively standard times and amounts rather than purely ad hoc smaller feedings throughout the day.

- If you wish to delay or avoid bottles, involve Dad in the before or after rituals of each nursing session when he's home. Couples often share by having Dad bring the baby to Mom, change the diaper before or after, or handle the burping and rocking.

- Share feeding duties based on the natural sleep needs of each parent. Some couples find that Mom is a night owl and Dad is an early riser (or vice versa) and have orchestrated their evening/night/early-morning duties around those characteristics.

- Don't use paternity leave time primarily for Dad to do housework and run errands. Early babycare days are precious opportunities for him to take full responsibility of his new baby, so give him as much time to do so as possible—maybe even with you out of the house. One ESP couple sent Mom to the library for several hours each afternoon.

- If you will be transitioning to formula after an initial breastfeeding period (or will not breastfeed at all), build shared feeding duties directly into your plans.

- Give Dad the lead on solid feeding. Once your baby begins to eat solids, Dad is home free. Many fathers who wish to share equally in their children's care say that they are happy when this day arrives.

Aside from breastfeeding, *maternity leave* itself is another big trap for inequality because it can establish us as fully responsible for our babies right away. Does this mean sacrificing our leaves? Not at all. But it does mean being conscious of the effect that maternity leave has on equal parenting, and correcting any noticeable inequality as soon as possible. Consider, for example, coming up with creative ways for your husband to intermingle vacation days with your time at home, and carving out lots of time for him to experience solo parenting. It may feel easier to just do all the work yourself at first and worry about equality later on, but you will have a mountain to climb as you undo unequal patterns—and your baby, that cute creature of habit, may not take kindly to the hike, never mind your husband.

The darker side of the responsibility myth is the idea that mothers are *better* at childcare than fathers. Happily, no one can prove that mothers (or fathers) are inherently superior to their counterparts at raising their children. Yet the idea persists, and it is up to us to reject it with confidence. We can do this by trusting in our partner's competence or at least in his ability to learn right along with us. Phrases like "you're doing it wrong" or "I told you so" don't belong in an ESP mom's vocabulary, lest she wish to end her equal arrangement. In fact, belief by either partner that one is inherently better at parenting than the other is a deal breaker for equally shared parenting.

The depth of letting go that must happen to achieve equal responsibility is often underappreciated. Take your typical over-worked, do-it-all mom who handles the majority of childcare responsibilities and is critical of her husband's way of dressing, bathing, feeding, or otherwise caring for their children. She thinks she's better at all these activities, and she often has direct proof in the shoddy job he does when she lets him take over occasionally. She would be absolutely right, but that's because she never really lets go. Even when he's at the childcare helm, she's there to clean up anything he "forgets" or bungles as soon as she's back on duty—and reinforce her supposed superiority. A man (or any adult) who is given false freedom to parent equally will have no need to rise to the occasion.

We can learn to stop taking on more than our share of child-care responsibilities in many small ways. For instance, try alternating which parent supervises bath time, jointly planning the kids' birthday parties, and trading off duties when both of you are available (e.g., if the lawn needs mowing and the baby needs his lunch, don't just assume you'll be the one dishing out the strained peas).

Here are some other tips from ESP couples on how Moms can let go of childraising work and responsibility to make room for sharing these evenly with their partners:

- During your maternity leave, intentionally save some childcare activities (bathing, nail clipping) for your partner when he returns from work.

- Don't denigrate his parenting style or skills to others, or directly to him.

- Don't bail him out when things get tough on his watch. He is as capable as you. One ESP father credits his full indoctrination into parenthood with the time he had to single-handedly wrestle two screaming toddlers as his preschooler whacked the television with a spoonful of peanut butter. He now owns the memory of resolving that little incident all by himself.

- Don't remind him what to do (beyond relaying essential facts) or consider it necessary to prepare anything for him when you leave him alone with the kids.

- Make sure you know which parent is "on" with the kids when you are all home so that no one swoops in when the other is in charge, or you both don't think the other is handling their needs.

- Alternate responding to nighttime awakenings for comfort. Marc once overheard a new father admit that he didn't hear his baby's cries when his wife was home but was up all night, listening to every snuffle and sigh, when she had to go out of town. Selective hearing doesn't need to be gendered!

- Switch off which of you gets to sit next to your baby (or toddler) and function as what one ESP couple calls the "primary dinner parent" for meals at home or in a restaurant.

- When you feel the urge to "correct" his way of handling the kids, frame your comments so that you're talking to a true peer. One ESP mom innocently asks, "Have you noticed that [XYZ] works for handling [Childcare Issue A]?" rather than states, "Let me tell you what I know about [Childcare Issue A]." One method sets the scene for two equals conspiring to come up with the best solution; the other assumes one of you has superior knowledge.

Rights

So far, our job as ESP moms includes rejecting the ideas that "Mom's the boss" (territory) and "children are women's work" (work) or "Mother knows best" (responsibility). Our final task is to deal with a mother's tendency to claim first dibs on the emotional joys of parenthood. Put another way, we have to let go of the argument that "Mother is more important." Problems sur-rounding maternal rights typically take two forms—*privilege* and *gatekeeping*.

The bond between a mother and her offspring is often ele-vated to the level of the sacred Madonna and child. No similar glory is attributed to fathers and their children, and this discrep-ancy leads us right down the path of *privilege*—or, as one ESP mother prefers to say, "Holy Motherhood Syndrome." Consider how an audience member on *The Oprah Show* (January 23, 2007) responds to her decision to stay home at the end of her maternity leave instead of returning to work as planned:

> When she was born, I just—our eyes looked at each other and I fell in love. And I feel bad that I'm kind of bailing out on my husband and my plan of what we had wanted to do, but I just looked at her, and I instantly changed.

This type of thinking is sweet and understandable on one level but allows a woman to invoke her societal privilege and sentence her husband to sole breadwinning and apprentice parenting. Most of us can easily imagine a new mom saying these words, but we would find it highly unlikely (and rather presumptuous) for a new father to make this decision for himself—regardless of his wife's wishes—instead. Why? Because we're told that mothers have this right and fathers don't.

Gatekeeping can be seen when women are threatened by their partners' involvement with the kids, or when they actively prevent this involvement or closeness from reaching a threatening level. It is fairly obvious to see gatekeeping behavior in the mother who insists "her" daughter must have snuggles from Mommy rather than Daddy at bedtime or that "her" son only wants Mommy to make a boo-boo better. But sometimes gatekeeping can be less obvious; it can look culturally normal, even as it conveys an underlying message that a mother is always the Favorite Parent.

Melissa and Rudd, a Watertown, Massachusetts, ESP couple, offer a story that illustrates an absence of gatekeeping. Their son, then one year old, had his first big fall on Rudd's watch, when he rolled off the changing table and landed facedown on the floor. Melissa was home and described the scene: "I heard him fall and start crying. He had blood all over him. I fetched a washcloth just to be helpful, and Rudd did all the fixing and comforting. Luckily he got a bloody nose and that was it. Anytime your child is hurt, there is an instinct to pick him up and comfort him, but I knew that Rudd had him and that was fine."

Even in a time of crisis (or potential crisis), Melissa knew that Rudd's role as father was just as important as hers and truly understood that this incident could have happened in her care, too. She wasn't play-acting equality when times were serene, only to rush to her son's side and take over as his comforter and savior when the going got rough. She didn't judge her husband's parenting skills or intentions, or rob him of the experience of fully caring for his son's injury, or send her son a signal that Mommy should be the parent of choice when he really needs one.

Recognizing maternal privilege and gatekeeping lets us see them for what they are—self-defense tactics that reflect the emotional needs of the mother rather than her bigger wish to give the best to her child. But parenting should be about our kids, not us. It is the child who has the rights here, the right to be cared for and loved by both parents—period. Despite my discomfort, this is what I felt when Maia chose Marc for hugs after she fell off that swing. Or as ESP mom Helena says of her husband, "My biggest fear is that I'll die before my kids are grown up, so I don't want them to be completely dependent on me. I want their father to be able to do everything I do." Whether out of fear for their safety or joy for their abundance of father presence, an ESP mom is able to replace her wish to be the sole center of her children's world with her desire to give them a fantastic team of loving parents.

ESP parents share rights to the pride of parenthood all the time. Here are some other ideas from moms we've interviewed:

- When friends come to coo over your new baby, don't claim any more credit or parental attention than the baby's father. One lesbian ESP couple calls this avoiding the "Bio-Mom Power Grab," and took specific care to equalize the attention paid to them upon the birth of their daughter.

- Similarly, give your husband public credit for his childcare moves when applicable. ESP mom Kitt recalls a moment at a party when her toddler got hopelessly messy and she whisked him off for a fresh change of clothes; another mom remarked, "Good thing Mommy packed extra pants." But it was Daddy who had done so, and Kitt readily admitted it.

- Don't use your mother or mother-in-law as your new baby's second parent. Prioritize time that your husband gets with the baby over time anyone else (except you, in equal measure) gets with him or her. This includes Grandpa, too, of course.

- Purposefully invest time and energy in non-child-related interests/hobbies, and continue to value your career, so that you don't form your identity too closely around motherhood alone.

- Equally share controllable baby "firsts" (such as first solids, first Halloween, and first trip to the zoo—and even later, notable events, such as the first visit from the Tooth Fairy).

- When you have a second child, don't automatically take the baby and give your husband most of the responsibility for the older child. Despite breastfeeding practicalities, spread the joy of each child between you both as much as possible.

- Don't automatically put yourself in charge of parenting when the public rewards are the highest—such as hosting your child's birthday party or bringing him to school on his first day of kindergarten. Share these joys, or take turns experiencing them. Your husband has an equal right to be seen in public as the representative parent.

- Ride out those twinges of anxiety that you've given away your motherhood. ESP mom Angela remembers when her six-month-old was nursing poorly and rejecting her affection in favor of her partner's. *I could have been The Mom*, she remembers feeling. She tried out the primary-parent role for a while to assuage her fears and quickly realized that sharing was much better. "The grass wasn't greener. The perks of sharing to my marriage, my own balanced life, and my daughter became crystal clear."

In an equally sharing family, moms and dads have equivalent access to the experiences that lead to intimacy with their children: perhaps Mommy-and-me music classes, Daddy-and-me daily walks, or alternating parents responding to nighttime calls for comfort. In any case, ESP parents embrace the notion that motherhood is not more important—more sacred—than fatherhood.

What's a mother to do? Recognizing, rejecting, and replacing these traps of inequality—territory, work, responsibility, and

---

EQUALITY CHECK: HOW TO LET GO

All of this letting go sounds great on paper, but it can be terrifying when one tries to put it into practice. I'm supposed to "let" Marc dress the kids without even a subtle hint that red plaid doesn't go with orange flowers, or that it is 20 degrees out and they need undershirts? I'm not supposed to undo the damage after Marc gets soap in the kids' eyes during bath time? I'm supposed to be okay with Marc feeding them fish sticks for three meals in a row? It is so easy to step in, fix things, take over. And so hard to refrain—not just on the surface by not speaking or doing, but on the inside by not even thinking that mine is the better way.

Abdicating control, or power, doesn't mean that you hand all control over to your spouse. It means that overall both of you—the team—are in control. Really give your partner space to do things his way. If he screws up, he'll take responsibility by dealing with the results and learning differently. If nothing untoward occurs, you're the one who learns the lesson. If the discomfort remains, it is time for a team discussion—without judgment by either party—so that you can come up with the Family Rules for specific situations together. Otherwise, watch your husband excel at fatherhood.

rights—are all part of the hard work required to achieve ESP. You can't have it both ways. Society has ingrained in us that a mother is the Chief Parent, but you can't have an equal partner in raising your children if you make all the purchasing and childcare decisions, take care of all the things your kids need, and go on believing—be it consciously or subconsciously—that your way of parenting is best. ESP calls on all of us to truly trust and believe in our partners.

Okay, it's now time to switch gears—and genders. I'll step aside and Marc will look at childraising equality from a man's perspective. . . .

Stepping In: Equal Childraising for Fathers

Don't worry, guys. This section is not a plea to pay more attention to your wife's parenting advice or lighten her load. My assumption is that you are willing to do your share of childcare and that you probably pitch in plenty already. You probably wouldn't be reading this book if that weren't the case. However, if your dream of a happy marriage includes a deep connection with your partner as you share the everyday adventure of childraising, and an equally intimate relationship with your children, then I invite you to stick around for a discussion of your part in equal childraising because you just might like what I have to say.

The question here is one we've asked of numerous ESP couples over the last couple of years: How do men not only become equal partners in raising their children but fully enjoy doing so? Their answers, and mine, are remarkably similar. Our culture sees fathers as backup parents, with primary duties that take them away from their children and out into the world. This leaves us guys with three tasks that will get us to full first-response-parent status:

1. Be available.
2. Be competent.
3. Be yourself.

Be Available

It's no secret that if you are working crazy hours and traveling extensively while your wife takes care of the kids, then you are not equally sharing childcare. However, as you move toward equalizing time on the job with your wife's work schedule (we'll cover this in the next chapter), it gets easier to see how you could even out the time you each spend caring for your children and your comparative level of involvement in their lives. Just as for ESP mothers, our goal as fathers is to share fully in the work, responsibility, and power of childraising with our partners—through equal time and effort—and to build a balanced life that includes all the joys and challenges of parenthood.

It would be impossible, not to mention arrogant, for me—or anyone—to parse out the hours of the day into a single, clean solution that balances childcare duties for every family at all times. The strategies used for equal childraising by ESP couples are as diverse as the individuals. But ESP dads all agree that carving time out of your life for the kids is essential to getting to the really "good stuff" of fatherhood—not just attending a few soccer games or taking a couple days off when your baby is born, but participating on a consistent basis on par with your wife's involvement. No need to choose between quality and quantity time—

ESP fathers believe in striving for both. But regardless of how much time you (and your partner) ultimately arrange with your children, the idea is to fully engage in the experience.

David is an Arlington, Massachusetts, ESP dad who owned his decision to spend time with his children and took steps to make it happen. David worked full-time as an analyst for a government agency when his wife, Andrea, became pregnant with twins. Shortly before the birth, he had a life-changing talk with a manager at a different, more family-friendly agency—a man who was courting David to fill an open position and had a vision of work-life balance that extended to the male gender. "He really opened up my eyes to the challenges of being a parent, and the importance of a flexible and supportive work environment," David said. He accepted a job from his parenting mentor and was granted approval to change his weekly schedule to four 10-hour days. He also received permission to take his paternity leave as one day per week over a few months instead of as a block of time when the babies were first born. After Andrea returned to work, David was home alone with his new babies two full weekdays every week.

The decision to make a time investment in childraising is the first step to becoming an ESP dad. Actually attaining equal childcare time between you and your partner can be an elusive goal. For many couples, being equally available is something they work toward in small steps rather than jumping in all at once as David did. It may mean asking for a small change in your work schedule (e.g., the chance to leave early on Tuesdays in exchange for starting early on Fridays), turning down a promotion that would require more hours at work, or scaling back your hobbies. Or you could simply start by making yourself more available to your kids during the hours you're already home. ESP dads describe how they tend to get their children involved in projects around the house—cooking with them, raking leaves with them, biking to the store with them. One ESP dad made a game out of trips to the grocery store with his kids, for example, drawing out the grocery list in picture form and sending them down the aisles in search of the needed items. Even when our children are babies, it is amazing what can be done while they snuggle in that front carrier: wash the car, return phone calls or email, go for a walk, load the dishwasher. Here are some other ideas ESP dads have used for building lots of time with the kids into their schedules:

- As a new father, take the time off from work that is available to you, or that you can afford—paternity leave, vacation time, FMLA time.

- Consider delaying when friends and family are allowed to stop by to see your new baby. When visitors do arrive, greet them as two equal parents.

- Don't use your job as an excuse to miss hanging out with your baby in the middle of the night. As one ESP father said, "I only had to sleepwalk through a few months of work, but if I had skipped this stage, I would have felt like I was sleepwalking through fatherhood instead." Another told us that he would not have traded those magical moments of holding his baby all alone in the dark—just he and his little child rocking close in the stillness—for anything.

- Join a playgroup or a babysitting co-op. This can set the expectation that you'll be the parent involved in these activities, and give you a chunk of time to be with your kids on a regular basis.

THE CASE FOR EQUAL PATERNITY LEAVE

I f you've just welcomed your first baby into the world, chances are your partner was able to arrange a maternity leave to spend her days with him right away. Apart from time to recover from childbirth and to breastfeed, ESP parents maintain that you have an equal right to the same time to bond with your new family member. Many employers don't make it easy for you to take extended paternity leave, which is almost always unpaid. And yes, there are often significant social and job performance pressures on men not to take time off to care for a baby. But if you want this level of equality right from the start, you must navigate past as many of these barriers as possible.

Many ESP couples point to their ability to arrange for equivalent paternity leaves as a huge reason why they were so successful in creating childraising equality for the long haul—especially if paternity leave is taken "solo," meaning once your spouse has gone back to work. It's a great shortcut to instant ESP, and delays the day when you'll need to begin outside childcare. It can even make a shortened maternity leave acceptable, as exemplified by Andrea, the ESP mom of twins, who could return to work part-time at six weeks without worrying, because her husband, David, stayed home on the days she worked.

So if you're thinking of giving up income for your spouse to extend her leave, consider taking that extra time home instead—as a single block or in days parsed out over multiple months. When in doubt about your rights to take leave from work, ask! You will certainly be able to achieve ESP over time without an initial parental leave that matches your wife's, but we've never known a guy who has taken it to look back in regret.

Be Competent

Getting motivated to spend time with our kids would be a no-brainer if it was all easy stuff like trips to the zoo, baseball games, frolicking in the yard, or rolling around with a giggling baby. But of course we know this isn't reality—we're not stupid! We've been hearing moms try to convince us to do more childcare for years by telling us how lonely, demanding, and tiring it is. They may want to work on their sales pitch, but I digress. If you're going to take on half of this "burden," you will probably want a decent return on your investment. Let's even shoot for enjoyable and meaningful.

I've met many men who love their kids, but deep down, they dread the prospect of long stretches of time alone with them. These fathers get through those hours or days without major harm to anyone but describe the experience as a survival exercise— ranging from total boredom during extended pretend play to frustration when a toddler refuses to nap or eat anything Mommy didn't make. But what happens when these men commit to becoming more complete fathers? The change is mostly in their heads—an internal shift toward valuing their role as a nurturer. ESP dads give up assuming they don't have to excel at childcare because their wives will always be there to do a better job. They participate in the establishment of routines, develop an arsenal of child-pleasing activities, and learn to build some structure into a day at home with kids. They reach to become experts in far more than the physical tasks of childcare, and strive to actually be there when they are home as opposed to just punching the clock until their kids are in bed.

This mentality requires you to ignore the common tough guy warning of "don't get too good at it or you'll be expected to do more." I never much cared for this perspective and actually think it goes against our very nature. Nowhere else in a man's life does ineptitude pay dividends—not on the job, not in sports, not in the bedroom. The path to enjoying any activity is through the process of getting good at it. Getting competent at the full range of fathering responsibilities is a move taken directly from the ESP equality playbook; equal responsibility means equal competence, and competence leads to pride in your contributions and feeling great about your place in the family. And this leads to all the rest of the good stuff—including really knowing your kids inside and out, and letting them into your head so that they come to know you just as well.

If you want to be an equal partner in raising your children (and other areas of your life) and reap all the benefits, I suggest you roll up your sleeves, flex your muscles, and learn all about your kids. Go ahead, change their diapers, jump into pretend play, discipline when needed, establish healthy eating habits, soothe your crying baby, debrief your kindergartner about her day, talk about sex with your teenager—and then do it all again until you can do it with confidence.

Here are some other childcare skill-building ideas that ESP dads have shared with us:

- Attend childbirth education classes with your wife. Ask questions.

- Right after your baby is born, take advantage of the experts all around you—nurses, physicians, lactation specialists, midwives—who can teach you how to care for him or her. One ESP father tells of a wise nurse who showed him how to bathe his new daughter in the hospital, and then proclaimed him capable of teaching his wife what he'd just learned.

- Become a guru in one or two specific little aspects of childraising; this will instantly elevate your status to uber-competent and give you confidence in your overall parenting skills. One ESP dad became known for his legendary swaddling prowess; he quickly became *the* bedtime comforter for each of his babies and has since demonstrated his "baby origami" technique to many other new parents.

- Take charge of your baby for a full day every week starting early on (even if it has to be a weekend day) to ensure your competence. If your partner asks you later why you did something with the baby a certain way, you'll have a real answer. You'll be able to hold up your end of the conversation and perhaps even teach her some of your tricks.

- Venture out alone with your kids—shopping, restaurants, children's museums, visits with friends. When you go, take charge of packing all the supplies you'll need for the adventure.

- Learn about children's clothing and shoe sizes, and shop for these items as needed.

- Go to the pediatrician with your baby alone, at least sometimes. Later, add the dentist to your solo-parenting repertoire.

- Get involved at your child's school by signing up to chaperone a field trip, chair the playground committee, or volunteer to help out with a classroom project.

- Take charge of a lasting part of your children's education. Multiple ESP fathers we've met have taken responsibility for raising bilingual children, patiently and consistently teaching them their own native language.

Think you can't do something as well as your wife does? Prove yourself wrong! Adopt the attitude of one ESP father who emphatically states, "I have no interest in being a second-rate parent." In addition to all the possible benefits to your kids, you get to be true to yourself. I would suggest that competence is bliss; leave ignorance and dread to those who are afraid to succeed.

Be Yourself

I have to admit that I feel sorry for guys who must defer to their wives' parenting rules. It's not pretty, especially in public, when an otherwise proud, successful, involved dad is reprimanded for not doing things Mom's way. That is how it goes when Mom is in charge. But when you are as available to your kids as your wife is, and you understand just as well how to care for them, you have earned the right to have your opinions weighed equally. Your job here is to stand up for yourself.

Amy and I like to tell the story of when our desire to equally share childraising was really put to the test. It happened on the morning Amy returned to work from her first maternity leave. She had carefully planned for this day, orchestrating Maia's schedule of feedings and naps over the weeks leading up to it. Just before heading out the door, she presented me with handwritten instructions for how much milk to warm for each feeding, Maia's expected nap times, and other specifics. I looked at the list only long enough to recognize it as my marching orders, and then tore it up right in front of her. I told her I knew what to do and could handle things without a reminder from her. My intent, although shocking to Amy, was not malicious, but I knew that I had to stand up for myself in clear terms. We both see the incident as a turning point. Even though I had been involved in so much of Maia's care while Amy was on leave, this was the moment in which I would be considered either a coparent or a substitute until the "real" authority got back home.

Not all couples face what we like to call ESP's Seminal Moment. But for many of us, there will come a time when fathers must defend their status as equal partners. Let's say a couple differs in their approach to their children's safety when crossing the street. Mom might want a rule that the kids must hold a parent's hand in all circumstances, and Dad may feel that this approach overprotects the kids and robs them of the opportunity to learn how to safely cross untethered on quiet streets. If this father worked lots of hours and his wife did the majority of the childcare, his wishes could get marginalized if not mostly ignored. But if they are equal partners, Dad's opinion carries equal weight— and rightly so. The kids benefit from the best ideas of both parents, and Dad is not relegated to an apprentice role with his own children.

With the mind-set that fathers are full parents in their own right, we are free to become our own *type* of parent—time with Daddy should be different from time with Mommy. We ESP dads don't just accept our wives' rules about whether our kids are ready to go down the slide by themselves or swing on the big-kid swings; we question and experiment, and must be trusted to do so. We love our children just as much as their mothers love them—only we do so as fathers.

Here are some other hints from ESP dads on how to proudly find your own parenting style:

- Develop your own innocently quirky ways of accomplishing tasks with the kids. One ESP father involves his kids in folding the family's laundry by dumping it in a big pile in the living room and letting them jump in the clothes first. He also happily allows them to brush their teeth in the kitchen sink full of dirty dishes. Neither practice is his wife's preferred way, but it works.

- Be true to your intuitions when you play with your kids. ESP father Bruce loved to go for spontaneous adventures with his son when he was small and found that most moms around him were focused on ticking off scheduled tasks instead. He found another father and son duo, and together they made the best of many beautiful, sunny days.

- Be proud of your full participation in parenthood when talking to other men. You are not a victim of your wife's coercion; embrace this fact.

- Don't let your kids dictate which parent does what around the house. If Johnny wants only Mommy to put him to bed every night, don't cave in. He may object for a short while, but he will eventually enjoy special bedtime routines with both of you, and you will all benefit.

- Respect how your parenting style differs from your partner's, and believe in your kids' ability to understand that their parents are two distinct human beings.

If we dads want to share equally in raising our children, our job becomes recognizing and rejecting our culture's standard (and rather low) expectations of fatherhood. We must take joy in making ourselves available, competent, and true to our own parenting beliefs and style, and reject such follies as hiding behind career pulls, feigned stupidity, or the helper role. We must resist comparison to "other fathers" and focus on our own full involvement. We can succeed by jumping eagerly into every aspect of parenting—stepping up to coparent status and becoming willing to fight for it if necessary.

Putting It Together

Once you have confirmed your commitment to equal childraising as a team and become aware of what each of you must do to steer clear of gender assumptions in your parenting roles, there is still a bit more to tackle to reach a childraising partnership: the daily logistics. This means working together on three ongoing team projects:

1. Creating a unified plan for parenting
2. Sharing the tasks of childraising
3. Learning to communicate as equals

Creating a Unified Plan

On the surface this may sound like Parenting 101, but it is critical for both parents in an ESP couple to be working off the same set of rules—not just for the kids' sake but for your sanity as parents. Even though each parent has free rein to practice his or her own style of handling the kids, the two of you *together* are directing the show. Of course you both separately have the best of intentions, and there is often nothing wrong with showing the kids two ways of doing things. But if you notice an issue in which two different parenting approaches are actually sending mixed messages to your kids, it's time to come up with a unified plan B—together.

Let's say you each have a weekday afternoon at home alone with your two elementary school children. Dad likes them to get their homework done before any TV is watched. Mom, on the other hand, enjoys giving them some downtime after school before they start in on their homework. Creating a unified plan will involve some delicate discussions that allow each parent's philosophy to be heard and balanced against the merits of his or her partner's wishes. The resulting family rule for after-school activities, for example, can then be owned by both parents and will keep you both on the same team. And just when the plan seems to be working like a charm, your kids will wake you from your peaceful and smug utopia—and you'll get busy cooking up another unified plan.

Sharing the Tasks

There is no perfect way to divide up childraising tasks, and perfection is not the goal. The real goal is to each spend about the same amount of time caring for and actively raising your children. You can piece this together any way that works for both of you.

With the repetitive newborn responsibilities of diapering,

feeding, and comforting, for example, you might consider dividing up the tasks by chunks of time—say, she handles everything about babycare two evenings a week, he does another two, and you both share the remaining three evenings together. Or perhaps, as we divided things for a time, one of you might handle all night awakenings before 2:00 a.m., and the other take over for any later wails. We had some laughs hoping that our children would stay asleep during our respective "shifts"!

When children are older, many ESP couples tell us that they alternate the bedtime wind-down (toothbrushing, pajamas, marching kids to their rooms) and morning routine (waking, clothes on, breakfast, and toothbrushing) every other day. This keeps them both actively involved in their kids' lives, and gives the kids a predictable dose of both Mom and Dad on a daily basis. The kids often remind their parents whose turn it is to do what! This technique can also be used to tone down rather than magnify phases during which a child prefers one parent. Still other ESP couples adore doing these activities as a parenting pair, and choose to forgo efficiency for guaranteed family togetherness. One couple even religiously doted on their firstborn through his nightly bath, and then each read alternating pages of his bedtime story; when their second child was born, they quickly realized it made more sense to divide some of this instead!

Activities can be delineated by interest, practical availability, or whim, but we caution you not to divide them by so-called aptitude—a slippery slope back to one parent owning all of a given task. They can be wholly divided, fully shared, or mostly done by one parent; we also advocate minimizing an absolute division so that each of you remains capable of every task and so your children see both of you as being equally competent. To get you thinking, we have created a list of some common childraising responsibilities at the end of the chapter. No fear—you don't need to carefully divide each task or even discuss most of the items on the list. It is simply meant as a tool to help you consider all that goes into caring for your kids, so that you can step back and assess your current sharing, identify areas where you both want to make a change to enhance overall equality, and revisit how you're doing from time to time. Because just as with a unified plan, your division of labor will require constant tweaking as your children grow and their needs change.

Learning to Communicate

You will need to communicate on a consistent basis to renew and revisit your commitment to equal childraising, and to unify your approach and decide how you will share the tasks. But the talking isn't over when these things are going well. In a traditional marriage, Mom has little need to tell Dad about the birthday party their son is attending on Friday afternoon because she'll probably be handling all the details—buying the gift, responding to the invitation, driving him there, and picking him up. But in an ESP family, both parents need to know just about everything, often in specific detail. This may seem daunting, but we're here to tell you that it is worth it, and that it gets fairly easy and automatic after a short time. We call it the "dance of ESP" because it becomes a smooth passing of information back and forth, with very few missteps.

In our house, the big picture is handled through an online family calendar that we both update. We sync the calendar with our cell phones and agree verbally before scheduling playdates, swim classes, or other activities for the kids. Routine daily logistics don't require as much discussion as one might suspect because we build our sharing around an informal schedule. On any given night, for example, we know who is responsible for each child's bedtime routine, who is cleaning up after dinner, and who is packing lunches for the next day. In the evening after the kids are

ESP AND OLDER CHILDREN

At ages seven and four, our children still require our presence for bedtime and baths. Though we are far from the dreaded teenage years, we know they are coming, and we've learned that they can bring fresh challenges to an ESP home. While some ESP couples tackle teen concerns in true team fashion, others find their equality particularly challenged by their different strengths in approaching the needs of young adolescents.

Once children are older, the old ways to split the childraising duties—sharing the diapering, feeding, and rocking—are no longer valid. As many ESP couples find, these are replaced by the need to focus on sharing emotional nurturing. Watertown, Massachusetts, ESP couple Sharon and Jonathan, whose two daughters have since left home, felt this shift firsthand. "The teenage years were messy—volatile, intense, and trying," says Sharon. Jonathan, who had been a competent and active ESP father to his kids throughout their childhood, suddenly found that he "felt at a loss about how to keep the intimacy I'd had with my daughters as they became teenagers who necessarily needed to pull away. They clearly didn't want me to play with them anymore, and I had to respect that. It took me a while to come to terms with my new parenting role when all I could see I was doing was driving them around. In retrospect, I wish I could have seen that coming sooner and understood better what I had to offer them in those years."

"Watch your childraising equality over time!" these parents of older children warn us by their stories. Push yourselves to grow competent in new areas, just as your children are doing.

in bed, we usually debrief each other about the day for a few minutes, discussing any parenting issues that arose for either of us in order to present a unified front to the kids the next day.

Equally Shared Childraising in Action

When the two of you come together to practice equally shared childraising, you will experience something sublimely different from tradition. The magic of an ESP arrangement is felt by each of you—and by your children. Two competent, involved parents personify the old adage that two heads are better than one. You get to model best practices for each other while watching and learning how to become more adept in those situations in which you don't excel. This can have the effect of turning both of you into better parents if you're open to the learning, and we believe it can dilute the imprint of your individual neuroses (we all have them!) on your children.

For mothers, equal parenting brings freedom—the ability to leave the house at any time without worrying that the kids are in substandard paternal care, the sharing of the anxieties of parenthood with a full partner, the relief from full decision-making responsibility in child-related issues, the sharing of childcare tasks and their tedium.

For fathers, ESP gives you the ability to know your children on your own terms—intimately and continuously. You get to share the joys and struggles of parenting more closely with your wife, leading to a connected partnership. You can take your kids' excitement and appetite for learning back into your career, and embrace family time as a necessary ingredient for a happy life.

We are not here to claim that equally shared childraising will create smarter, more obedient, or better-looking children. In fact, we can assure you that as you move closer to an ESP arrangement, your kids will still throw tantrums and challenge your authority—as they should. What we aim to convey is that equal childraising works if you both want it, and sharing this domain is particularly worth the effort. When we raise our children together equally, we are parenting with pride and joy. We give them our best selves—our greatest gifts—when we learn from each other how to be most effective with them. And we give ourselves and each other the gift of balance and partnership along this miraculous journey.

Childraising Tasks

In deciding how to share childraising tasks, keep in mind the ESP goal of an overall balance of time and involvement between partners rather than equality for each individual task. Consider the following activities (and others) in your analysis:

Assembling toys/equipment

Bathing children

Celebration planning (birthday party, christening, bar mitzvah, graduation, etc.)

Childcare and babysitter coordination

Clothes purchases for children (including deciding what to buy)

Clothes rotation (seasonal availability, removing too small items, storing too large items, giving/accepting hand-me-downs)

Crafts, projects, and other activities

Diapering, toilet training, and bathroom supervision

Discipline

Emotional care of kids (during day hours)

Extracurricular classes/sports/camps (attending or providing transportation)

Extracurricular classes/sports/camps (selection and enrollment)

Feeding children (including breastfeeding and bottle feeding)

Homeschooling

Homework supervision/assistance

Medical/dental care for children (making appointments, accompanying them)

Middle-of-night care of kids (soothing from nightmares, cleaning up bedwetting, etc.)

Morning routines (getting dressed, hair combing/styling, brushing teeth)

Nighttime and nap routines

Nonschool learning supervision/assistance (help with piano practice, etc.)

Packing children's supplies for vacations or day trips

Packing lunches and other items for school/camp

Playdate/playgroup/other social activity coordination

Playing with kids

Preparation for feeding children (cooking, preparing bottles)

Present purchases for children (your own and their friends)

School drop-offs and pickups

Sick child care

Supply purchases for children (diapers, wipes, school supplies, toothpaste, etc.)

Taking time off from work for childcare needs

Teaching your children things (how to ride a bike, read, cook, etc.)

Volunteering at school

Career

MORE THAN A JOB/LESS THAN YOUR LIFE

Equally sharing the family breadwinning is probably the gutsiest of the four domains of ESP. In evenly distributing the workload of childraising and, as we'll cover later, the housework and time for individual pursuits, a couple has only to work things out between themselves. But in sharing the work of maintaining a career and bringing in the money, we have to fit our lives to outside requirements as well—company policies, acceptance by managers and peers, and the logistical demands of any job. So much appears out of our control! It is clearly easiest for a couple to fit equally into the working world if both parents accept inflexible full-time-plus jobs and schedules (and perhaps even matching long commutes), and maybe see each other and their children briefly in the evenings. This scenario plays out daily in plenty of homes and could qualify for some as career equality. But does it provide for satisfying, balanced lives?

Or consider the outside forces at work when couples give up on career equality altogether—in the name of pure, immediate financial logic, and in order to bend to corporate pressure for the "ideal worker."* Here, we find it fascinating—and unfortunate— that so many couples automatically compare the cost of outside childcare to only one parent's salary. This practice omits so much that could be considered in the "who stays home" discussion. It assumes that a job is just a paycheck, it places all the family's financial eggs in one basket, and it doesn't take each partner's short-term and long-term happiness or future earning potential into consideration. Who says a cardiologist or a lawyer can't find a way to match a spouse's work hours? It may be tough to arrange, but we challenge you to prove it can't be done! Who says a nurse or secretary can't contribute *enough* to the family, especially if she doesn't have to withstand a résumé gap and if she works out a shared plan with her husband that lessens their daycare expenses?

Remember that ESP asks us to reach for equality in each domain of life. And it also calls for the equal goal of balance. So, we need to jack up the expectations one more notch—to create not only a partnership of *two* working parents but two *balanced* lives that each fit work into its proper place, all while playing by the rules of our business culture.

---

*The term "ideal worker," meaning one who works at least forty hours per week year-round, was first described by Joan Williams in her book *Unbending Gender: Why Family and Work Conflict and What to Do About It* (New York: Oxford University Press, 2000). As a parent, this type of worker, by definition, must rely on others (typically a stay-at-home or marginalized-career spouse) to care for his or her children when they are sick, have early-release days from school, and so on.

Just as childraising defines mothers in our society, breadwinning is the meat-and-potatoes of manhood; equally sharing the career domain is therefore an exercise in upending how we think of "real" men. ESP asks men to remake themselves from the inside out—not ending up in a full reversal of roles, such as in stay-at-home-fatherhood, but in a connected, balanced and equal partnership with their wives. Women, as a generality, have a slightly different assignment. In a culture that gives a mother permission to bow out of paid work (individual finances permitting), ESP mothers must reject this offer and uphold their responsibility as full-fledged family breadwinners.

Before we further address these challenges by gender, however, we want to talk about an unconventional way of viewing our jobs and careers—one that connects directly with the philosophy of ESP.

The Artisanal Worker

Central to a standard career mentality is the belief that we're always working to *get somewhere else*. This job will prepare us for the next one. Our current title will be replaced by a loftier one if we play our cards right—network with the right people, jump at the right opportunities, and prove ourselves along the way. We might aspire to become managers, or rise to greater responsibilities or more power in some other way. Even academic tenure doesn't mean a permanent career plateau for most, since we're always encouraged to jockey for ever greater prestige compared to others in our field. Conventional wisdom says we should carefully strategize our way to the good life, viewing each step as simply that: a temporary state or a means to some end. But this habit of always looking ahead to the next career move has a way of preventing us from noticing that life could be pretty good at any stop along the way.

If we're living a life in balance, so that we've got time for everything that matters most, we can free ourselves to make choices based on more than what we guess will make us happy in the future. This paradigm shift allows us to *love our job right now* and is at the center of what empowers the ESP couple to truly share the career domain. It is a shift toward what we call the mentality of an *artisanal worker*.

Artisans—masters of fine woodworking, lauded musicians, or gifted writers, for example—work hard to learn their trade and become extremely good at it. They cherish what they do, and this attitude shows in their craftsmanship; their self-worth on the job comes from their dedication to excellence rather than from any outward praise (although they likely receive plenty). Now let's expand the classic depiction of an artisan beyond the world-class artiste. One can be an artisan at anything—plumbing, teaching, managing, waiting tables, even handling complaints at an insurance company. As artisanal workers, we can give to the world by our experience, our expertise and passion, and our sincere effort to do any job well. We can enjoy our work solely for the doing of the work itself—not because it's a stepping stone (even if it turns out to be) or a means to justify our place in the world. And in general, we are able to build a reputation as thoughtful and present workers as a side product of our genuine love for our work.

A hallmark of the artisanal work ethic is *getting good at your job*—an investment that can pay off later, although not in the way you might think. It is no longer true that this strategy automatically guarantees you a steady climb up the standard corporate ladder until retirement. Yet the artisanal worker is poised to understand that the true beauty of early effort is simply *personal expertise, skill, and reputation.* An apprentice plumber brings home a modest wage, for example, but a master plumber with a reputation for efficient, high-quality work can make far more money in far less time. Working efficiently and establishing yourself as an excellent, loyal, and artisanal employee in your twenties, for example, can pay dividends later when you're ready to scale back and make room in your life for marriage and parenthood. Your value is a known commodity that any employer would be lucky to snag. And you can entertain the possibility of working less for the same take-home pay as someone less "valuable." You can make the trade-offs that ESP couples so often make and have a good chance of earning enough to live comfortably. Instead of using your résumé to climb higher, you can use it to work smarter!

Jan and Saskia are an ESP couple who live in Haarlem, the Netherlands, and share the care of their two-year-old son, Manu. When Manu was born, Saskia stayed at home only eight weeks before returning part-time to her job as a project leader for a government institution that supports volunteerism. Jan, a freelance sound engineer for theatrical shows throughout the country, took a full eight months off to care for Manu shortly after his birth, and then began to accept jobs once again—now only on a part-time basis just like Saskia. Today, Mondays are Daddy Days for Manu, Tuesdays he spends with his grandparents, Thursdays he's with Saskia, and he goes to daycare for the remaining two weekdays. Both parents' jobs take up three to four days each week. Jan worked hard before he became a parent to build his reputation as an ace sound guy, and he now says, "I can choose my clients, and I go with the ones who pay well and demand fewer hours. If there's a band tour that needs someone six to seven days every week, I'll ask about bringing a colleague on the job. If they say no, I won't accept the gig."

Saskia and Jan love what they do and have developed solid reputations in their fields. Yet neither is focused on the classic corporate climb toward the next tier of success, and as a result, they are able to retain equally important careers and balance them with the rest of their lives. They have used their expertise as a means to bring in fully adequate, albeit not maximal, paychecks. We have noticed similar thinking in many of the ESP couples we've met—such as Tara and Brian, who have run their own karate studio together in Watertown, Massachusetts, for seventeen years and happily passed up many opportunities to expand their business in favor of time with their two children, or Liz and David, the two-physician couple from Pittsburgh, Pennsylvania, who both feel energized by 50 percent work schedules that allow them to share the care of their four children (even homeschooling them).

But what about the idea that young workers don't want to remain in one job, or even one career, forever? Some ESP parents are content with their lives as masters of one profession, especially if they have spent many years training to get there, but many of us want a varied dose of adventure on our résumés. This wish fits equally well with the artisanal worker mentality if we regard our "craft" not as the specific field of work we do but as our *dedication to excellence* in the job at hand. Artisanal workers love their work, whatever that may be at the moment. Today, you may be a middle manager or a trumpet player (or both), and next year you may follow your dreams to be a sculptor instead. But ESP asks you to focus your love on the work in front of you, to become fantastic at it, and then to move on as necessary, with awareness that *too* much job-hopping will diminish your ability to excel—

and interfere with your capacity to stay devoted to the present job. You can polish your skills as a manager, flex your lips as a trumpeter, or hone your creativity as a sculptor, and relish your work in any form.

Being an artisanal worker can seem like heresy. We've been taught to think ahead to the next opportunity rather than double-down on the one we already have in front of us. Some of us are concerned about looking stagnant if we stay in one position too long, and of course, none of us wants the résumé scar of a backward career move. So many of us keep stepping up until our lives and skills aren't as suited to what we do, or until we've traded prestige and money for the parts of work we really enjoyed, or we burn out, retire, or die. At any point, any one of us could get knocked out of this rat race altogether—through a layoff, a disability, or some other catastrophe. But we're expected to keep climbing nonetheless, and to do otherwise can feel risky.

Your challenge in creating equal careers is to be ready to live differently. We're not asking you to quit your perfectly lucrative job to become a goat farmer in the mountains of Vermont. But almost all the ESP couples we've met have let go, in their minds, of the need to steadily climb the career ladder. This is because they've discovered that when they do, the world opens up. They can enjoy where they are. They thrive on doing their best on the job every day. And instead of fighting to be noticed for the next promotion, big break, or pay raise, they're free to use their leverage to fight for the work schedule, hours, or commute that balances their career with all the other things that make up a happy life. The fear of taking risks lessens, and power increases.

Let's turn now to the issues that typically arise as each gender works toward equal breadwinning.

A New Identity:
Equal Breadwinning for Men

The challenge in the career domain for ESP men (and also many women) is to let go of an ingrained job-as-identity thinking. You can love your job, enjoy the time you devote to it, and even bask in the glory of your successes, but you don't have to let this become all-consuming. You are so much more than what you do at work; you're also a father, husband, son, neighbor, friend. Without this whole view of yourself, sharing breadwinning with your wife can feel like a loss of who you are. By expanding the lens through which you view yourself, you can become free from the sole, or even the primary, burden of providing your family's income. You can share the depths of this responsibility with your partner.

Likewise, it is difficult to make room for other parts of life if you are compelled to keep pushing forward in the one way that defines you. But pursuing a balanced life offers a sustainable alternative to solely identifying with your career. Whether you ever take action, or would even want to, a balanced career perspective gives you the realization that you *could* find a way to break away from any job (or any profession) if it prevented you from being happy. To an ESP father, no job, paycheck, or worldly reputation is worth years (or decades) of sacrificing yourself, or your relationship with your partner or your children, or even a meaningful connection with your home.

John and his wife, Annie, share equally in raising their three children, ages eight, six, and two. John was an aerospace engineer at NASA in Houston and Annie worked in a nonprofit agency when they had their first child. But when they welcomed their second baby two years later, she quit to do some freelance writing from home and John took on the primary breadwinner role (now expanded to frequent 60-plus-hour weeks as a result of the Space Shuttle Columbia disaster). It soon became clear that neither John nor Annie was happy with this arrangement. So John tested the iron rules of his government employer and approached his supervisor for more flexibility, while Annie began a master's program to pursue her career passion for international humanitarian work. Thus began a series of unorthodox job hours for John— and even a one-year telecommuting stint—made possible by a generous boss and extremely hard work. But it all came to an end when John got a new supervisor who forbade such flexibility.

Having tasted the life of flexible work, John didn't want to return to the grind of long hours in the office and little time to see his children. John's "moment of understanding" came the day his supervisor refused his request to leave early to coach his kids' soccer practice. "The bubble had burst, and we could see clearly how we wanted to live," John recalls. He and Annie decided they would like to have a third child, and John gathered the courage to make his move. He left the security of a good government job and the astronaut career track to enroll in an environmental engineering PhD program in New York City, and Annie continued graduate study toward her own PhD at the same university. They moved across the country.

Now several years into their doctoral programs, John and Annie are both happy. As John describes, "The important thing is that we now have our ideal life. It's not easy to make ends meet on a grad student's salary, but at least nobody can tell me I can't see my kids. I know that eventually we will both graduate and need to find a new home for our unique arrangement, but at least I have the renewed confidence of standing up to the work-first system—surviving and thriving in spite of the system's rejection of our values. When we do go back to more traditional jobs, it will have to be on our terms, or we'll just say, 'No thanks, we have more important things in our life right now!'" Annie emphasizes what will sustain them: "We feel so, so lucky. Gratitude for our warm, shared family life is the backbone of everything we do."

THE FALSE BENEFACTOR

Society might praise a man for being generous if he tells his wife, "Honey, I'm happy to support whatever you want to do—you can have a career if you want to, or I'll take care of things if you want to stay home." But in reality, his message says that his career is the real one. His wife's career is just a little pet project; optional, nice to have, not really that important. The outward result of such an attitude may look like equality, but inside relationships like this, men are retaining the upper hand in the career domain.

What happens when there's a school cancellation for snow? When he has a business trip? When she has one at the same time? When they have to negotiate who works longer hours on a given week and who prepares dinner for the kids? When the school nurse calls? When the kids need a ride to dance lessons or the school play is at 1:30 p.m. on Wednesday? When he gets an offer to move out of state for a promotion? Mom's job gets kicked to the curb, over and over.

Then what happens when Mom's paycheck looks rather slim after her career has been marginalized for a while, all while her husband's job has been skyrocketing in importance and pay because he's had the time to devote to it? Mom realizes that her salary barely covers daycare. She reverses her decision to stay in the workforce—benevolent as it was of her husband to provide it—and stays home after all.

We paint an extreme picture (although not uncommon). But you get the point. The "gift" of supporting your wife's less-important career is no gift to ESP.

Many of us would find it hard to do what John did in jeopardizing his career without an equally lucrative plan in sight. And we're not suggesting such a move is ever necessary. But as an ESP man, you will need to work with your wife to craft a fantastic career for yourself (while she does likewise) beyond the typical path of maximizing your income and worldly status. As most mothers know all too well, maintaining your career is more challenging if you are asked to keep it in perspective with childraising (and the other areas of your life). Often, a man's career is either untouched by fatherhood or even enhanced by the prestige and practicality of having a wife who cares for his children and hosts his business clients. This gender advantage is no longer yours with ESP, however. We must *all* step up to take our own share of the baby punch on our careers. With pleasure.

Your Right Arm: Equal Breadwinning for Women

In many ways, women have the easier task in this domain; your challenge is to step up to equal breadwinning status. You've got lots of company in the working world. Women have been wage earners with full careers for decades, and we can thank a first-wave feminist for paving the way. Women may not yet garner the same paycheck as men for the same work (especially once they become mothers),[2] and they may find themselves outnumbered at a conference of Fortune 500 CEOs—both complex and frustrating issues that merit focus elsewhere—but they do have considerable opportunities to earn their way nonetheless. Women are also collectively much farther along than men when it comes to figuring out clever ways to balance work schedules with the needs of their children. The workplace sometimes makes this horribly hard to do—still—but you're not looked at with complete disbelief if you claim motherhood as an excuse not to work yourself to death. A mom who wants flexibility at work is at least a known commodity.

With respect to equal sharing, however, you do have some work in your pile. Foremost, you have to believe, just as strongly as any man, that breadwinning is your responsibility. Even when the going gets rough—you hate your job, you miss your kids, you can't find a good daycare situation, you get laid off or fired—you have to avoid pulling the rip cord labeled "I'm staying home." Other solutions exist, and you must (together with your partner) explore them fully. Perhaps a nanny search is in order if the local daycares don't cut muster—or a transition to no outside childcare at all if you can both work your schedules to make this happen. Maybe you'd be better off with a completely new job or field of work—no matter how many job interviews, refresher classes, or training seminars you have to attend. Certainly you can focus on the reality that your kids benefit from more than your own physical presence—that your husband's presence is just as valuable; maybe, then, you can work part-time and make room for your spouse to do the same. All these solutions and many more are acceptable—just no throwing in the towel. Careers for ESP mothers are as important as their right arms. They are equally responsible along with their partners for bringing in the family paycheck, and their goal is equivalent hours spent earning it.

Even a crummy salary is not an excuse for opting out of the workforce. We all know a mother who now stays home with her kids because she and her husband compared her salary to his. He's a lawyer; she's a secretary. Or he's a doctor, and she's a nurse. His salary could more than pay for their expenses, but the cost of daycare isn't much less than her annual paycheck—taking taxes and other deductions into account. There is nothing, however, about equally shared breadwinning that specifies equal salaries. Making about the same amount of money as your husband just makes ESP simpler and more logical to the outsider. But the spirit of ESP has plenty of room for partners with widely different paychecks, different projected lifetime earnings, and occupations with different social statuses. In fact, pushing past these differences is all the more crucial if you want any decent shot at an equal partnership, since they so typically lead to rampant *in*equality—first on the job, then at home and with the kids.

Debby and Carl are an example of ESP breadwinning that triumphed over a seemingly logical, but unequal, financial solution. Parenthood started out pretty traditionally for this couple from Saskatoon, Canada, with Debby on maternity leave from her job as a clinical psychologist and Carl continuing to work full-time as a newly tenured professor of psychology. But Debby and Carl deliberated long and hard about their career plans until they ran a little experiment. Debby granted Carl a full week at home alone with their four-month-old daughter. The experiment changed their perspective—and their lives.

Debby negotiated a return to her field in a new half-time job, while Carl weighed the best path for him to achieve similar hours. Because a half-time faculty position provided poor benefits and sabbatical allowance at the time, and with the knowledge that an academic job in his field was hard to keep to specific limited hours, Carl resigned from the university and took a half-time clinical job in a hospital. As a result, this couple sacrificed Carl's coveted university tenure and spent the next eleven years raising their two daughters as equal parents and equal breadwinners. Debby maintained her career as a psychologist, varying her work hours as their children grew. Eventually, Carl started over as a probationary faculty member at the same university and attained tenure again much later. Today, Debby and Carl's daughters have left home to live their own dreams, and this couple looks back on their decision with not one morsel of regret. Their memories of sharing what mattered most outshine everything.

At the time, some of Carl's university colleagues thought he was nuts. And perhaps some of your friends will think you are crazy as well. But like Debby and Carl, and all other ESP couples, you can choose to secure your financial future by diversifying into two income streams and prioritizing equal opportunities for fulfillment for both of you. Your big assignment as a woman is simply to sidestep the cultural signals that tell you your job or career is less important, or that you have the right to opt out of breadwinning on an equal involvement level with your husband. And of course, the same concept of equality also applies if you make *more* money than your partner, or have a career that might be more lucrative than his down the road.

Bending Both Careers Half as Much

When you become a parent, a whole new life domain is born— your opportunity to begin sharing childraising. To make room, both of you will have to shave off time from other domains, often including breadwinning. Adjusting your work life is accomplished by claiming your share of all the strategies long employed by new working mothers—now applied here to both genders in an ESP family. The good news for ESP couples is that each of you will typically have to make much smaller work changes than one parent is called to make in a traditional arrangement. And small changes can make a big difference when you and your partner are working as a team. For example, you can think about the option to:

- **Shift your current work hours.** One of you could start work an hour or two earlier, and the other could begin a couple of hours later. This gives you both a bit of juicy solo-parenting time every day. Commuting time may also be shorter during off-hours.

- **Compress your workweek.** Work four 10-hour days per week. If both of you can do this, you've reduced outside childcare needs down to three (albeit long) days each week. Combine this with staggered hours and you can even cut those childcare days down to regular length. By the way, we are not advocating against outside childcare per se; this and other options can significantly reduce childcare expenses and limit outside care for those parents who prefer to do so.

- **Work from home.** Reduce commuting time and gain the freedom to schedule your workday around a bit of bonding time with your kids. If only *one* of you telecommutes, however, be watchful that this scenario doesn't introduce some inequalities in your housework and childraising responsibilities.

- **Reduce your hours.** Our favorite! Probably the most commonly used method of balancing work/family in ESP families. Combine a slight reduction in hours (say, to thirty to thirty-five hours per week)

with a staggered schedule and a compressed workweek, and the possibilities really open up.

- **Become self-employed.** Another common tactic.
  Self-employment provides a means to flexible work
  and balance if you are then self-directed toward ESP.

- **Work on an academic or seasonal calendar.** Teach-
  ers, gardeners, housepainters, and sports coaches
  can share breadwinning in a cyclical manner, taking
  more of the work hours during their busy season and
  more childraising during their off-season.

- **Work a different shift.** Plenty of couples manage to
  avoid any outside childcare by working opposite
  shifts or days (including weekends). If not combined
  with reduced hours, however, this can be tough on
  your time together as a couple and as a family, and
  on your ability to find time for yourself.

Marco, the ESP father in Petaluma, is an example of ingenu-
ity in job flexibility. Ask him about his work as a high school
history and English teacher and he replies in a voice that sparkles
with enthusiasm. This is a man who truly loves his job. Yet when
his first daughter was born, he was the only employee of either
gender (the school was relatively new) to request parental leave—
granted at three weeks with full pay just because he asked. He
repeated the request when his twins were born and now shares
equally in the care of all three children with his wife, Megan.

Along the way, Marco experimented with his role at the
school. He accepted a position with quasi-administrative respon-

sibilities for a time, but soon realized his true love was classroom teaching; he quickly relinquished this responsibility (despite the fact that it came with a stipend) and returned to what fit him best. Recently, Marco noticed he was feeling stressed with the workload at home and at school, and took advantage of his job seniority to negotiate his current reduced-hours position at two-thirds' time. He now teaches in the afternoons and spends the mornings with his kids. "My new schedule takes the edge off and gives me just the right balance—more time at home, enough time in the classroom, and time for all the 'other things,'" he explains.

Many women approach their post-motherhood careers in this manner, but as Marco's career path illustrates, *men* can and do use the ideas above—and others—to mold jobs they love to the lives they want. Which approach appeals to you the most? Do you find yourself mentally crossing off one after another? It will take a combination of desire and imagination to see how your job could work in a way that doesn't appear possible now. Yes, you can admit defeat and live out your career in a standard work schedule that doesn't fit well with your ideal life. But if you want something different—and believe in the payoff for the pain you might endure to get there—you might be pleasantly surprised to discover how much power you truly wield. We will talk about ways to approach your boss and make unconventional work arrangements successful in the next section. But for just a moment, let the focus be on you. So think big, crazy, brilliant thoughts. Or if you can't even begin to fathom a work change, start by experimenting; take some available time (vacation days, sabbatical time if applicable, certainly your owed maternity or paternity leave) to think things through. ESP dads, in particular, often share with us

THE ALMIGHTY FORTY-HOUR WORKWEEK

Somewhere along the line, we were told that a full-time job takes forty hours a week. It has become the all-powerful 1.0 full-time equivalent (FTE) in a manager's budget and the right minimum number of hours to ask every full-time employee, by default, to work.

But the problem comes when we take this business measure and assign it a social value—if, for example, we feel less important in a job posted at thirty-nine hours per week. At just a couple of water cooler breaks' difference, we're all of a sudden the dreaded "part-timers"—slackers who are no longer devoted to our jobs. How foolish! In an ideal world, we would all be paid by the results we produce regardless of how long it takes us to do our work. We'd be highly motivated to work efficiently so that we could skip out of work early (or do more if we truly love to spend our time working).

ESP couples often characterize themselves as efficient—sometimes even boasting that they do full-time work in a fraction of the time it takes everyone else they know to do the same. Some work full-time hours but find ways to say no to even more work that will unbalance their lives. The lucky ones are actually paid full wages for standard full-time results at reduced hours. The rest of us take a pay cut if we want official rights to slightly fewer hours on the clock—and we push past the social stigma of doing so.

Don't allow yourself to be trapped by the necessity of fitting into the typical full-time job. ESP allows you to at least consider finding balance through working less—to consider thinking "outside the box" and putting in the effort to find or create a job, or transform your current position into one, that isn't tied to the magic threshold of forty hours. The right number of hours at work is the number that pays you enough and gives you enough time there. Maybe that's 1.0 FTE; maybe not.

that time spent delving into their family lives, or even a hobby or adventure, has helped them make an informed choice about how they want to spend their waking hours in the long run. Give yourself this token gift, at the least, so you can think bigger when you're ready. Your boss won't be all that excited to grant any request you don't want yourself. What'll it be?

Getting That Yes

After you have a good idea what your own ideal work schedule might look like, you are ready to explore the strategies that ESP couples use to actually get what they want from the work world. Let's start with the assumption that you've got a job you generally enjoy, but you would like to make a change in your schedule—perhaps work only four days a week or leave early on Tuesdays and Thursdays. How would you make that happen? There are many great resources that can guide you through these negotiations and help you keep your boss happy after he says yes. We've listed a couple of our favorite ones in "Additional Reading" at the back of the book. But here are the rules that have worked for other ESP couples:

Rule 1: Take full responsibility. It isn't your boss's job to figure out how to make your request work out; it's yours. Don't approach your boss for a meeting unless you've got a full plan that includes what you want to change about your schedule or responsibilities and, most important, how this change will be a positive one for your company. Don't just describe how it will keep *you* happy. Your argument must focus on the specifics about how your work will get done—well and on time—and how your new schedule will play out with your colleagues. If your plan involves a reduction in paid work hours, include this as a company benefit; the less your boss must pay you, especially if you can still handle most or all of your current duties, the happier he or she will be. Finally, ask for your job change with plenty of time left for your boss to think through the details of your plan; unnecessarily pressuring your boss to make a decision quickly is a sure way to sour the conversation.

Rule 2: Make no assumptions. Many dreams of flexible work die before they are ever heard. That's because the dreamer doesn't think they'd ever work. Once you believe in your ideal schedule yourself, you now have to sell it to your boss. So speak up. Don't assume your plan is impossible just because it hasn't been done before or even if it has been proposed a hundred times and rejected each time. If your proposal becomes the 101st rejection, retool your approach and ask again. And again, ask nicely. Your supervisor may be afraid that granting your request will cause him or her to permanently lose money in the department budget or make it impossible to rehire into your position if you quit. These are valid concerns, albeit unfortunate. Persist nonetheless, with a list of terrific reasons to chance these worries. Sometimes employers will allow flexible schedules or reduced hours on a temporary basis; take this offer and then build your case for continuing the arrangement permanently by showing everyone how well it is working.

Rule 3: Build up seniority. It costs a huge amount of money for most employers to let a well-trained worker go, recruit and establish another, and perhaps replace the new hire, too, if things don't work out. This concern is especially significant if you're a loyal, long-time employee who really knows the ropes. So, as long as you're not perceived as dead wood, seniority is a great thing for ESP work flexibility. It goes hand-in-hand with the artisanal worker concept, which leads to . . .

Rule 4: Be known as a stellar worker. Competent, helpful, and productive (and well-liked) employees are usually more likely to get what they want. So build a reputation for creativity, high-quality work, and service to others. Take responsibility for new projects or programs. Prove yourself worthy. Meet deadlines. Be cheerful. Don't complain without serious cause. Then, when you ask for a different schedule, your company will be more likely to take your request seriously. Your boss will know that losing you would be a huge blow. After you've been granted your new schedule, continue your dedication to demonstrate that the plan is going well for all.

Rule 5: Minimize the change. There is wiggle room in almost everyone's job for a little goofing off. In fact, studies show that close to two hours of an average person's eight-hour workday are actually wasted on surfing the Internet, gossiping with co-workers, staring into space, and dabbling in other nonproductive nothings.* By harnessing this knowledge, you might be able to maintain full-time productivity even if you reduce your hours (many ESP parents attest to this, such as Carl, who considers his part-time years among his most productive simply because he was happiest—and motivated to be especially efficient). Furthermore, office spies aside, most employees are more concerned with their own work than with policing yours. So the more unobtrusive you can be about your new schedule (and about asking for it), the better. Bring up the change only on a "need to know" basis in conversations at work. Continue to do your work on time, attend meetings, and respond to emails or calls whenever possible. Especially if you work in multiple locations, you might even be able to get away with very few people feeling the effects of your new work hours.

Rule 6: Remain flexible. Whatever you do, don't ask your man-

*Per the Wasting Time at Work Survey conducted annually on thousands of workers by Salary.com, 2005–2008. For more interesting statistics on time wasted at work, read details about these surveys at www.salary.com.

ager for flexibility without being willing to show your own flexibility, too! When negotiating, listen to your manager's concerns and try to address them within your plan. Be able to consider alternative plans that may work better for your company and still provide you with your balance and childraising needs. Are you absolutely needed at the weekly operations meeting? Rework your dream so that you can be there, but ask for a shortened schedule on another day of the week instead. Don't close off any option until you have considered it well. Then, after you assume your new schedule, remain open to tweaking it over time if necessary.

Rule 7: Stay available. As a reduced-hours or flex worker, you may not be perceived as available to take a business trip or come in off-hours to launch a major project. This should not be true! Volunteer for just such a task and let your boss know that if given enough advance notice, you can come in on occasional extra days. These opportunities will have to be worked out carefully with your spouse, of course, but can be done. By showing that you're a team player who makes sacrifices to pitch in when needed, you are reducing your chances of being marginalized at work. On your home days, connect with work via email or phone (if applicable) when your kids are napping or otherwise occupied, and respond to critical messages whenever possible. This will send the message that you have not checked out as a flex employee. If your boss begins to take advantage of your generosity, start to ask for compensation in return, such as taking a different day off if you have to come in on one of your usual home days. But in general, a little flexibility goes a long way; and the more flexible you can appear, the more your boss is likely to go to bat for you, and your coworkers will have nothing to complain about.

Rule 8: Know your benefits. Flexible work arrangements can wreak havoc on your healthcare or other benefits, especially if you also reduce your work hours—or so many of us assume. While we've heard many a horror story of employers who offer no healthcare coverage to any part-time worker, we've also known plenty of companies that provide decent coverage (albeit pro-rated, which we should expect) all the way down to a work schedule of twenty to twenty-five hours per week. Most of us don't read the fine print on our benefits packages, but now is the time to do just that. Would thirty-five hours still constitute full-time employment? What happens to each type of benefit at thirty-two or twenty-eight hours per week? Does your company offer paid maternity or paternity leave? When Maia's birth required cesarean delivery, we didn't realize that Marc's company offered the perk of two additional weeks off with pay as an enhancement of the Family and Medical Leave Act! We took advantage of this benefit when Theo was similarly born.

Getting That Yes from Day One

All of the above strategies, and others, make up your overall game plan for getting a yes from your current employer. But if you're in the market for a *new* job (perhaps because your current boss never gave you that yes), you'll need a few additional tricks. It can be difficult enough to find a job with the right pay and the right fit to your qualifications and interests—especially in a tough economy. Then heap on the pressure to find one with the right schedule, too?

Perhaps Marc's telling of his own story can help here:

For almost five years, I was the only man in my large corporation who worked part-time—three days per week (a total of twenty-seven hours). I truly enjoyed my position as a senior computer support technician until the day my whole department was outsourced to an IT support service, and I found myself—a guy in his early forties—in search of a brand-new part-time job.

I decided to use my job hunt as an opportunity to test the system, along with testing my dedication to a balanced life. Could I get an employer to pay me well for my experience and expertise, even though I wasn't interested in a full-time job? There were no postings for decent part-time jobs in my field, so at first I tried responding to publicly advertised full-time positions and recruiters with my résumé and a letter describing my desire for reduced hours. No luck.

I then used a more traditional cover letter—one that omitted mention of my preferred schedule. Right away, I got calls from interested managers and was able to arrange a number of interviews. I discussed my flexibility desires with those employers who seemed somewhat amenable. The consistent response was in defense of corporate policies of flexibility, but a firm explanation that *this* position was full-time, with little room for negotiation. Strike two.

I began to interview without mention of my wish for reduced hours. When I landed my first offer this way, however, negotiations broke down after I asked for a nonstandard schedule over the telephone. My potential boss, a man, was offended that my reason for a schedule change was to have more time with my children; he responded with a lecture about how he worked at least fifty to sixty hours per week but was a "very involved father." I had inadvertently put him on the defensive. He countered with an offer of more money—and I walked away.

I didn't give up. With my next job offer, I requested an in-person meeting to discuss the schedule and benefits. The meeting began with a reiteration by my would-be boss that the job was indeed full-time with a premium on being present during normal working hours. I acknowledged this and offered the understanding that he would be taking on some additional risk if he were to settle for less than the ideal candidate. However, I pointed out that every hire includes many risks. I stressed my qualifications and how I could meet the job requirements without working full-time, my stable work history, and my desire to find a job that fit into my life just as another employee might desire a different salary to fit a job to his financial needs. When he pinned me down to a specific schedule request, I gave him multiple options. He left me alone for about fifteen minutes while he discussed the offer with others, and then returned to accept the option that matched best with the company's needs. I agreed to adjust the salary offer down by the same percentage as the reduction in hours. Later, we confirmed how each of the company's available benefits would apply in my case, and I signed on.

Everyone's tale of sticking it out to find the right job schedule is unique. Each person's career, résumé, personality, location, competing applicant pool, and countless other factors play into the end result of any unusual job search. Either from a current job or from the ranks of the unemployed, however, it is possible to get what you want. It may take a long time and a lot of effort to find a company that you can get excited about working for and a boss who is willing to negotiate a flexible schedule with you. But having both partners on board at home to create the life you want makes all the difference. If Marc had not been able to find work before our finances were in serious trouble, we would have settled for something less than ideal. But that would have been a temporary fix as the job hunt continued.

Here are some tips from ESP parents who have faced tough challenges in looking for a new job that matched their lives:

- **Look for signs that a company is flex-friendly.** Do other parents (especially mothers) work there? Is anyone working flexible hours, telecommuting, or working part-time? What is the overall culture? If possible, get to know a few of your potential colleagues outside of a formal interview—and ask them what happens when they need to take off early and if they ever work from home.

- **Listen carefully to what constitutes the right job candidate.** Find ways to show your future boss that you're that candidate, so that your talents and experience can eclipse your unusual request for flexibility. Use what you learn to think up alternative ways to meet the job requirements while perhaps even saving the company money by paying a top-notch candidate a lower-than-normal salary for fewer hours worked.

- **Don't be afraid to look at standard full-time positions.** Not mentioning your wish for flexible or reduced hours until you receive an offer is no more dishonest than waiting until later in the interview process to ask for a higher salary or more vacation time. After the offer, too, you'll have a better idea of how to sell your plan as something that will perfectly meet the company's needs.

- **Know when to fold.** When you anticipate a job offer and know you'll need to broach the subject of flexibility, have a serious talk with your spouse so that you know exactly what it would take for you to walk away from the offer. Go into the final negotiations with a mental list of schedule options that you could accept so that you don't appear rigid, and so you can conduct yourself as someone who's ready to get past these negotiations and on with the job at hand.

Everyday Equal Breadwinning

Once you and your partner have achieved ESP job nirvana—gainful employment in positions you each enjoy, with approximately equal hours and schedules that allow for balanced lives—you'll need to keep it afloat. Equally shared breadwinning means sharing everything that goes into earning the family's money and tending two careers. Couples who succeed in doing this employ the following strategies:

- **Review schedules every week.** Since their families don't revolve around one primary breadwinner, most ESP couples find it useful to communicate the ins and outs of their workweek with each other. Some do this by sitting down every Sunday evening to go over the coming week's activities—who has evening meetings on what days, any after- or before-work appointments, the kids' school schedules, other social obligations. Some use an online or paper calendar to mark these items. Routine schedule review is also important to confirm which parent will be "on" which days for responsibilities involving the children or the home, and it avoids labeling one of you as sole keeper of the family's social calendar.

- **Minimize or improve commuting time.** Commuting can be a huge time sink, and an onerous commute is considered by many experts to be the number one reason for job unhappiness. ESP couples are often quite clever with their commutes—riding public transportation so they can get work done en route, or turning commutes into cherished exercise time by biking or walking. Many work from home to make commuting a nonissue. And many other ESP couples purposefully live close to work.

- **Keep your career time approximately equal.** By definition, equal breadwinning requires both partners to devote about the same number of hours per week (on average) to outside work. This is a loose but important goal, because your time at work directly impacts your partner's life and your overall equality. Equal work time includes all aspects of work lumped together—regular hours, commute time, overtime, "on call" duty, off-hours work, social obligations for work, business trips, and so on. It can even include time spent training for a career, whether at continuing education programs or in college or post-graduate courses, as long as your intention is to eventually use this training to bring in your share of the family income.

ESP couples sometimes find that keeping career time close to equal can be a challenge, not only from outside world influences but also from within the relationship. ESP mom Angela tells us that if left to her own devices, she could easily work fifty hours per week, while her partner, Dorea, could settle for a two-day workweek. But when they find themselves moving in this direction, they can tell that the balance in their relationship begins to suffer. As Angela puts it, "We feel we've truly dodged a bullet by correcting the course. We've learned to value putting the breaks on our opposite tendencies."

• **Keep your careers equally important.** In addition to equal time spent on the job, ESP couples strive for equal importance in the social structure of the family. Neither of you has a more important job, even if one of you works at the cutting edge of environmental research and the other is in food service. This means both of you have equal rights to request time to attend a professional conference, stay late at work on occasion, or ask the family to consider moving for an out-of-state job offer. The outside world will fight you on this one, but stay with your convictions that life is not only about making more money.

• **Trade off staying home with sick children.** Traditionally, Mom stays home when the kids are not well enough to attend school. This is not so in ESP families. Consider trading back and forth, or trading off this duty based on the day of the week; that way, there is no question about who is going to take the fall on which day. This can prevent a lot of battles and be appreciated by employers who then know that the other days are pretty much guaranteed workdays. Don't forget that as you reduce the number of days requiring outside childcare, you lessen the likelihood that *any* workdays will be used to care for sick children—one parent is often home anyway. Trade-offs can also be used to cover bad weather school cancellations or for events with plenty of warning, such as school vacation weeks, early dismissal days, in-school festivities, or parent-teacher conferences. Splitting the responsibility between parents evens the impact on spouses' careers.

It Isn't Luck

The universal cry of skepticism whenever shared breadwinning is discussed in traditional circles is the idea that ESP couples must just be lucky. They fall into piece-of-cake jobs with soft-hearted bosses who protect them from the harsh world of "real" employment. And in some cases, this is true. Some couples consider themselves lucky indeed, and anticipate that their particular work situations will eventually end. But we'd like to point out that the luck of any particular job schedule is no different from luck in any other aspect of life. Sometimes, we get lucky. Other times, not so much.

All ESP couples we've met agree that their lives are built on far more than luck. They've either been tested, just as we were with Marc's layoff, or they've begun to think about the eventual test to come. Or as ESP mom Liz puts it, "This is where the rubber meets the road. If I lost my great schedule, I'd take a job that wasn't as much fun before I'd take one that made me work more hours. Heck, we'd leave town if necessary to maintain our lifestyle." ESP couples almost universally live responsibly so that a job loss by one of them would not destroy their livelihood (we'll talk about this more in Chapter 8). They pay attention to the direction their careers are taking, so as not to get caught in jobs that threaten their balance and equality with extreme sacrifice required to extricate themselves. Or they plan ahead so that they can handle the financial sacrifice of one parent returning to school to train for a more flexible career or taking a pay cut to switch to a job in a completely different field. Many have tales of clashes with former bosses and of having won, then lost, then won again their right to a job that fits their lives. Many struggle each day to keep work at bay even after their supervisors have approved "reduced" responsibilities. But we have yet to meet an ESP couple who doesn't consider these struggles worth the effort, or who expects their equality and balanced lives to end forever once one of them loses a flexible job.

Equally shared breadwinning means purposefully choosing to optimize your life rather than maximize your paycheck. This mind-set acts as a beacon for ESP couples, and keeps them sane even in the face of uncertainty—impending job cuts, a tanking economy, or a glut of qualified younger workers. It also gives them courage to face outward scrutiny—judgment of a father's

THE END OF AMBITION?

When one parent pushes ahead with a power career—launching a political campaign for governor or gunning for partner in a top law firm, for example—traditional marriages afford that person plenty of time and energy to do this. But with ESP, the goal of balanced lives for both partners rarely allows this sort of career for either. Does this spell, as some have suggested, a double disaster—the end of good careers for both of you?

Ambition is a funny thing. Like money, it can take on a purpose of its own. And in our culture, ambition seems almost universally applied to our careers only. When do we stop and say "enough"? ESP gives us a different measure of ambition than classic outward career success. ESP couples are not less ambitious (many of them, like John and Annie, label themselves as "extraordinarily ambitious"); they do, however, define their goals in terms of achieving a happy life—through a meaningful career, a rewarding marriage, intimate relationships with their children, and the luxury of time.

Of course, we still need to preserve enough time for our careers to keep them solvent. So, does ESP prevent two careers from flourishing? We look around at the ESP couples we know to answer that question. We see an architect married to a web designer, an IT business engineer married to an IT project manager, a business analyst paired with a psychotherapist, an environmental consultant and a lawyer, dual clinical psychologists and dual physicians. In later chapters, you'll hear about ESP parents who work in programming, software engineering, nursing, mathematics, and other professions. Do any of these options sound shabby? All these people have made the career sacrifices that many of us may fear in pursuing this lifestyle, and they kept their perfectly appealing and lucrative careers all the same.

manliness by colleagues (and even by his own parents) for scaling back to be with his kids, or jealousy or even sabotage from coworkers not willing to make their own career changes.

It isn't easy in today's work world to simultaneously negotiate two flexible work schedules that mesh together! As an ESP couple, you *will* face an end to easy equal breadwinning at some point. You may even need to settle for a traditional, or reverse-traditional, job situation for a time while you regroup. But equal breadwinning functions on far more than luck.

Your Best Work

More than anything, equally sharing the career domain comes down to perseverance and courage. You and your partner are a team that won't take no for an answer. It can sometimes feel like you are locked in battle with the outside world. Fortunately, the business case for flexible work is becoming clearer—especially in a downturned economy. Employers are beginning to realize the wisdom of using reduced or compressed hours to avoid layoffs, and offering nonstandard work schedules to recruit and retain top-performing talent. Forward-thinking employers can also tailor their benefit structure to lose nothing (or very little) by offering reduced benefits to these employees.

We must all do the important work of guiding companies and our government to make flexible, meaningful work commonly available. But in the meantime, we are also compelled to take *personal* control of how we work—both in courageously seeking out jobs that can bring us (and our partners) happiness and in loving the work we do each step along the way. Working to earn a living is more than that. Our contributions to our chosen field or workplace lift us up as individuals and give us purpose beyond our own families. With an artisanal worker view, we can give back to our communities by what we do at work—with love and dedication. But work is not the sum total of our lives, either. It is not our only purpose, despite how workplaces tend to treat our kids as just pieces of paper in a frame on our desks or in our wallets, our spouses as just characters who show up at holiday parties, and our outside hobbies as just something we talk about in order not to appear too much like losers. While some companies boast of outfitting conference rooms with pool tables and offering free laundry service or gourmet meals to their hotshot workers so that their lives can be even *more* connected to their place of work, we must remember the folly of work-as-life.

Of course, our work is important. Yes, our employers should get the very best of us while we're there. In an ESP relationship, work is a vital, energizing, giving function that neither parent gives up nor lets overtake all the wonder of time spent elsewhere. The message to employers is no longer "pay me more money and I'll work longer and harder." It is now "pay me fairly, let me fit my job into my life, and I'll do great work for you."

Home

A MAN'S CASTLE/A WOMAN'S SANCTUARY

Sometimes you have to work backward to solve a good puzzle, especially if the solution has eluded many others before you. Such is the case when cracking the code on equally sharing the housework. There is important work you must do before you decide who does the laundry and who does the dishes, lest you fall into the classic traps of inequality lying in wait for you.

Disparities in housework have eroded many a marriage, and countless couples live with that toxic mixture of fury and guilt brought on by failed attempts to share the chores that pile up day after day. One reason that the housework-sharing dilemma remains alive is that it is hard to address when there is always something else "more" important to divert our attention. Who wants to spend time and energy solving issues like the dirty socks on the floor when you have dire money problems or one of your kids is doing poorly in school? But creating and tending an equitable relationship around housework is a fundamental part of ESP. Sharing the housework nourishes your life together so that you are capable of handling the bigger issues. Being willing to guard against dismissing the issue is vital to creating a true partnership. There's a lot at stake here.

For years, women have been trying to get men to do more around the house. Statistics are collected regularly to show how many hours of housework each gender does, on average, across America.[3] Battles wage over whether we should celebrate our slow but steady progress toward housework gender equality, or mourn the fact that we can't seem to speed it up. We know that badgering and finger pointing to force men (or women, for that matter) into housework equality isn't a good long-term solution. But what's perhaps less obvious is that we won't get there by simply dividing up the chores like mature adults, either.

Many couples try just that. And it works for a while, but then something interesting happens. One person doesn't live up to the other's expectations of cleanliness. One person starts to take over a chore in order to ensure it will be done "right." One doesn't notice something needs to be done until the other is seething with frustration. Oh, and don't forget that our culture plays a role in this unraveling, by reflecting the state of the home on a woman's worth, expecting her to handle the bulk of the housework and rewarding her partner every time he lifts a finger to help. So sooner or later, except in the rarest of couples, imbalance reigns.

In the interest of working backward to solve this puzzle, we will start by talking about what you *shouldn't* do if you want to reach harmonious sharing of your household chores. Then we'll go over a new approach that includes just two "easy" steps: *jointly defining the tasks* that need to be done in your home, and then, only after you both own the definitions, *sharing the work.*

Let's get down to the details—and equally sharing housework is very much about the details.

How *Not* to Share Housework

There are oh so many ways to get trapped in housework inequality! Role models from our parents' generation, a spouse who comes to the relationship with zero experience in the kitchen, personal housekeeping styles (or lack thereof)—these things and many more can unconsciously set couples up for a lifetime of imbalance around the home. Even without resorting to overt hostility toward your beloved's supposed laziness, it is easy to fall into patterns that don't get either of you where you want to be. We see four common mistakes at the root of most failures to happily—and lastingly—share the chores:

Mistake 1: Hold on to the job. "Whenever I let my husband clean the bathroom, he does a horrible job. So I take over again." "There is no way he'd spontaneously vacuum. He just doesn't see the dirt." "If I didn't bug him to take out the trash, it simply wouldn't get done." Or occasionally, "I love her to death, but she's a total slob. I end up spending my weekends cleaning up the place." These are the laments of the well-meaning alpha homemaker who doesn't notice that she or he plays an equal role in destroying housework sharing.

The issue here is control. As innocent as it might sound to bail our partners out by gently reminding them their chores await, showing them how a job should be done, quietly doing it for them, correcting their mistakes, or rescuing them from a task gone bad, all of these actions say "I'm still watching." We must stop imparting our unsolicited knowledge on them when it comes to properly loading a dishwasher, using a power drill, or slicing an onion. We need to quit nagging them if they don't get something done by deadline. We have to refrain from taking over in frustration—sending them the clear message that they aren't up to the job. In other words, we must learn to mind our own business. This is the housework domain's directive of equal power, a key component of ESP equality.

We get what we deserve when we stay in control. We get the additional burden of parenting a fully grown human. But we can also get a spouse who eventually gives up trying because it just isn't fun to be labeled "wrong" so often (or because he or she has started to believe us), and we can breed alienation in our relationships rather than intimacy. If you want something different, you will need to commit yourself to think of your partner exactly the way you hopefully think of yourself—as someone who will ask questions when necessary, makes mistakes that don't get labeled as signs of incompetence, and generally wants to succeed.

Natural consequences are your best friend in helping you let go. You can use them to do the dirty work that you might be tempted to do. Suspect your husband will shrink your jeans when he does the laundry? Say nothing. No eye rolling and no sarcasm when the jeans now fit your six-year-old, no getting huffy or blaming him, and absolutely no taking over the task. Or perhaps there are now no clean plates because your wife forgot *again* that she's supposed to wash the dishes? Let her be the one to explain to the kids that dinner is delayed while she scrambles to wash them—or enjoy eating on paper plates or right from the pan if necessary—but don't just label her a failure and bail her out. Let her make things right (even if that means asking you for assistance). This allows the responsibility to remain where it should—on your partner's shoulders.

If you can avoid a negative "I told you so" attitude that still conveys that you're superior, your inaction is actually a loving gesture that speaks of trust and equality. The person you've chosen to spend your life with is not dumb; he or she will know far better what went wrong in the laundry room or the kitchen if left to learn from personal mistakes—without having you to blame for pointing them out. The motivation to learn for next time can set in all on its own this way. If your other half needs further incentive to learn better laundry techniques or time management, the impact on the family's clothing or dining budget might do it. By the way, if your fears turn out to be unfounded (your jeans remain properly sized or your kids don't care that dinner is five minutes late), you've learned something equally important!

Mistake 2: Refer to your partner as your helper. Another misguided approach to equal housework—perhaps less obvious than outright control—is to label your partner as your "helper." Women are notorious for saying, with the best of intentions, "My husband is great. He helps so much around the house," or, in frustration, "Honey, I could use a little help sometimes." No. This is the housework equivalent of asking a man to babysit his own kids. Equal partners aren't helpers—you each do work of your own accord, and you don't take orders from each other. This is not to say that you lay banana peels in each other's paths, of course. You assist each other as teammates rather than as director and staff. We all understand that people relegated to a helper role are usually far less invested in the outcome of their labor than those who direct them; this fact of nature certainly applies to the housework domain. Achieving equally shared housework requires respecting each other as equals—with equal say in how the housework is done—and trusting in each other's similar competence.

Of course, we could all use a little break from our responsibilities now and then. And because we love our partners and want them to be happy, it is natural to want to clear their to-do list on occasion. If it's her night to cook, imagine how great she would feel if she came home from work to find a healthy dinner waiting. How wonderful it would be if she hand-washed the car he'd been meaning to take to Scrub-a-Dub. These are gifts. They are unex-

---

THE HONEY-DO LIST

Advice to women on how to get their husbands to pitch in at home often includes the "honey-do" list (as in, "Honey, do the grocery shopping on your way home and then please do that load of laundry I set out for you"). We think of this as an example of how insidious inequality is in our culture. Sure, spelling out what must be done can avoid the need for mind reading by your spouse, but the typical "honey-do" list is nothing more than a directive from a boss to a subordinate. It's a visual version of the helper label. It says "I don't trust that you can figure this out on your own or that you'll manage if I don't spell it out in black and white." This tool has no place in the ESP home.

Some ESP couples do use written chore lists that they can *both* refer to for the tasks to be handled in the morning before work, in the evening before bed, over the weekend, or during the coming six months. The lists may even include which task is assigned to whom and deadlines for completion. And many ESP couples simply remind each other that things need doing—we're short on milk, we need to bring cupcakes to preschool next Thursday, and so on. The difference is that these notes are not hierarchical—they are jointly created or a call-out to the team at large rather than a sugarcoated chore list for dummies that still leaves one of you in charge. Save "honey-do" lists for those rare times when your partner actually asks you for one.

pected and heartfelt, with no ulterior motives or control implications. This kind of self-initiated help is highly encouraged—and very sexy.

Mistake 3: Act dumb. On the flip side, if you are the one whose housework skills are still in the steep phase of the learning curve, it is easy to slip into playing the underling who needs constant supervising. This will get you out of owning responsibility, perhaps, but at what price? You need a new approach. When your partner provides unsolicited advice, your response should be, "Thanks, but this one is mine to handle." If you actually do need information (Where are the extra towels kept? How much soap goes in the dishwasher?), go ahead and ask. But don't ask over and over. You are an adult who is fully capable of learning how to care for the home. Take notes, post up your own reminders, and really take charge. Don't lean on your partner to be your memory and reference manual, just as you would not ask your colleagues at work to remind you over and over how to use the department printer.

Once a task is yours, don't let it slip back to your partner because you've decided you can't do it perfectly. For decades, men in particular have been able to hide behind the "but you're better at it, honey" excuse, and women have been buying it. Women aren't innocent either, especially when it comes to "guy" things, such as snow shoveling, climbing up ladders, or even jumping in the driver's seat when the two of you are in the car together.

Sometimes, acting dumb when it comes to a specific task can be long engrained in our personalities. We can label ourselves—perhaps even with pride—as being unable to boil water or sew on a button. Deciding differently can be a big mental hurdle, but we have faith that we're all up to the task. After all, if someone offered any one of us a million dollars to tackle a job we had sworn that we didn't have the aptitude for—such as sewing curtains or cooking a pot roast—chances are we'd miraculously manage after a few tries.

Mistake 4: Forget about the big picture. One other rather obvious mistake—although it happens frequently—is to expect housework equality in a marriage that is not yet set up for equality in other domains, especially breadwinning. If your partner works full-time and you stay at home, it stands to reason that you should do significantly more housework! Equalizing the chores at home comes together naturally, fairly, and practically as you move closer to equality in the whole of your lives together. This is why a balanced life, and equal sharing between partners in all domains, is so vital to the success of ESP.

Let's leave the mistakes behind now, and get to the task at hand. . . .

Jointly Defining the Tasks

Sharing a willingness to treat each other as equals and agreeing to live up to your own competence set the right mental atmosphere for housework equality. But now you need to take the first step to make it real. We have come to the practical crux of equally shared housework: jointly defining the jobs themselves. Without mutual understanding and agreement about what it means to do a specific chore—what, when, how, how often, and whether it even needs doing at all—each of you continues to operate from your own housework expectations. Your life together can feel like a big compromise. Either your own standards are continually being undermined or you live with an uncomfortable feeling that you're constantly disappointing your partner. It is joint task definition that drills ESP down into the details of running the home. Do not skip this step.

Let's look at a common scenario. Two tired parents return home from their day at work. They gather the kids and go about getting through their evening of dinner, homework, baths, and the kids' bedtime routines. Up until this point, both parents are full participants in the family's evening drama. But with the pressing chores out of the way, Dad's now ready to relax. It has been a long day, he thinks, and he's pitched in plenty. He moves some stray toys from the middle of the room and deems the house clean enough. Anything left to do can wait. The couch beckons.

Mom, on the other hand, is just gearing up. She's got a long list of chores that she feels must be done in order to simply keep the house in "maintenance" mode—packing the kids' lunches for tomorrow, doing two loads of laundry so their daughter's favorite shirt and skirt are ready when she wakes, and putting away all the toys that line the room. She looks around. The kitchen her husband supposedly cleaned sports crumbs on the counter, pans in the sink. It's his job to take out the trash for early-morning pickup, and she knows that once he settles down to watch television, it just won't get done tonight.

What happens to this couple in their precious alone time together that evening? She fumes and stays up late checking off her list. He tunes her out so he can try to relax—confident that he did his part and annoyed that she's once again inventing things he needs to do or do better. What went wrong? They each knew their agreed-upon chores—he thought he'd reasonably straightened the kitchen and has every intention of taking out the trash eventually, and she was free to do her job of making the kids' lunches. Neither person is slacking off. But they forgot to talk about what it *means* to do these things—how clean is clean, when do they have to be done, what is included in each task?

Most couples at odds about these types of standards don't step back and talk about them neutrally. They typically complain about individual incidents of chore lapse or chalk each other off as hopeless, maybe even talking to others about their clueless/unhelpful/uptight spouse. Actually taking the time to come up with enduring definitions of household tasks is not something most of us assimilate in the "love conquers all" days of courtship. But think about the big picture—that seemingly small frustrations can play out day after day for months, years, and decades. The laundry your partner doesn't do to your liking or that you are silently expected to do to someone else's principles is not just today's dirty laundry (metaphorically and in reality). It represents the tenor of your daily existence as a couple. Alas, these issues don't go away if they aren't addressed in some manner, and talking about them calmly usually gets harder over time.

Freeburg, Pennsylvania, couple Silas and Catherine share in parenting their three-year-old son and infant daughter, and both tend academic careers in fiction writing and tackle the housework as a team. When it came to doing the dishes, however, tensions used to arise in their marriage because Catherine felt that Silas wasn't pulling his weight. After talking, they realized that Catherine preferred the sink to be empty between meals while Silas was perfectly happy to "just leave them for the morning." This discovery led to a joint effort to solve the problem rather than blame Silas for inaction. They came to appreciate that a clean sink was far more important to Catherine than the extra few minutes of evening leisure were to Silas, and they agreed together to adopt Catherine's dishwashing timeline whenever possible.

Silas easily says that Catherine, in turn, "adjusts plenty on other things."

Catherine and Silas used their mutual wish to share housework to stop their cycle of blame and confusion, and to create a joint definition of what "doing the dishes" really meant to them. After talking about it, they learned that their sticking point was the "when" of this chore. This gave them a framework to explain what mattered to each person and allowed them to decide together that Catherine's plan could work for both of them.

In creating these definitions, both of you are invited—maybe for the first time—to fully codetermine the way housework gets done. Although Catherine's dishwashing wishes were granted in this case, she didn't "win" the battle; one partner's ideas no longer routinely trump the other's. Because no two people ever have the exact same personal standards for all chores, arriving at a consensus will require you to examine what is really important. Do you really need to scrub the shower once a week, or could you be satisfied with once per month? Should doing the laundry include folding and putting it away? If your partner explains why removing shoes in the house means the world to her, maybe you can convince her of a new approach to arranging that Tupperware drawer that's driving you crazy. Making these decisions together is an act of love—and of tolerance and understanding. And from a logical standpoint, joint definitions eliminate confusion; with a unified understanding of a given chore, it becomes crystal clear what should be done, how often, and by what method. In the end, you'll have devised an unambiguous statement of where your family stands on the issues—of dishwashing, shower cleanliness, laundry, shoe wearing, or Tupperware management.

Joint chore definitions connect both of you so that the teeny-tiny (or not so teeny-tiny) arguments don't have to happen on a daily basis. Rolling up your sleeves and coming to an acceptable agreement ends the battle to push for your way. And if one partner strays from a definition on occasion, ESP couples say they aren't as apt to argue about the lapse as they were before a definition was determined; they both can see exceptions for what they are without taking offense. Defining the necessary details of specific tasks tackles the problem head on.

This may sound like a horrible amount of work! We won't lie to you—it does take some effort to arrive at some of the most crucial joint definitions. Happily, however, you don't have to analyze every task down to the molecular level. In fact, if you're like most ESP couples, *most chores won't require any conversation at all*; many of the jobs that go into running a home will be no-brainers when it comes to reaching consensus. Who really cares *how* the vacuuming gets done as long as it does? Well, somebody does, but most of us don't. If you know each other at all, you already know the tender spots in your housekeeping differences

SHIFTING EXPECTATIONS

It would be great if every couple got the joint definition for a chore down pat after one conversation. Just do your best, and keep the lines of communication open. If a decision is driving one partner crazy or not working for any reason, it is up for renegotiation at any time. It is not up for unilateral amendment, however. So if your joint plan to water the plants once a month is leading to dead foliage, speak up!

The best time to bring up a joint definition that should exist (or exists but isn't working) is anytime except when your partner has just handled that chore. Wait until later to discuss how "buying the groceries" should include checking to see what you're low on first—not just as he's returning without the milk and mayonnaise.

or where one of you is unhappy with the current division of labor.

Other than for dishwashing, according to ESP couples, negotiations tend to be needed most often for the following:

- Meal planning and grocery lists

- When to make kids' lunches and what to pack

WHAT'S IN IT FOR MEN?

Housework equality can sure sound like a great deal for the average woman. But why would any self-respecting man want to sign up for extra work? ESP dad Silas jumps into housework because "it just feels bad to be lazy." But the reasons go way beyond this noble motivation. Taking on half the housework promotes men from a status of "just lives here" to full partner in the home decision-making. If a man thinks that dusting more than once a year is a waste of time, his view holds equal weight in the discussions. He also gets a full vote on how the home is decorated—no more ending up with frilly Victorian curtains or couches when his preference runs to early monastic.

In addition, taking on a fair share of the chores creates autonomy. Without fear of being judged by his wife, an ESP guy is free to do things his own way (within the bounds of the applicable definitions). Feel like running the washing machine at 3:00 a.m.? Want to try out a cheaper laundry detergent? Have a ball!

Some men also find that they honestly enjoy doing their share of the household chores—even those typically done by women. "Doing housework lets me flex a different set of muscles," says one ESP dad. "It allows me to be a generalist in life, which is just what I want to be." And others like getting really good at some particular area of homecare—such as the ESP dad who is known as the Family Stain Remover and "keeps a chemistry lab in the basement" fully stocked to remove even Silly Putty from a blanket.

- General clutter level of the house (One couple agreed that on the wife's working days, she would come home to at least one room that was not in shambles. Her husband and the kids had lots of fun figuring out which room to choose each day, and made quick work of the cleanup just before her arrival.)

- How often to clean the bathroom, and what constitutes "clean"

At the end of the chapter, we've provided a longer list of common household chores to get you talking. As you read through the list, make note of the ones that trigger a reaction in either of you. These are the chores most likely to be worthy of discussion.

Notice that we have not yet discussed assigning specific tasks to a particular person. That's because, in theory, joint definitions should be set without regard to the individual given each task. This keeps both of you engaged in the definition-setting conversations, and allows for mixing up the assignments over time because they are mutually defined. In reality, couples are usually well aware of who carries the load for each chore, but the spirit of the discussion should not include this information. Once a task is assigned, or reassigned, each person can either meet or exceed its definitions. If the picky vacuumer gets most of this duty, he can feel free to surpass all expectations. But if the indifferent partner ends up with some vacuuming, she must only meet the couple's meaning of "good enough."

Sharing the Work

Once you have worked out your joint definitions for those tasks that require them, you're finally ready to think about who will do what. The bird's-eye view of ESP housework sharing is an equal amount of *time* and *involvement* (and *energy*) devoted to household tasks by both partners. As long as you each meet this goal on average, you can share the chores any way you want. Ideally, both of you will end up doing a nice balance of *essential tasks* (those that must be done each day, such as cooking) and *noncritical tasks* (those that can usually be put off until convenient, such as changing the bed sheets, organizing the closets, or trimming the bushes).

How you share any one task often depends simply on what makes sense for your family. This is a slight departure from our warnings in the childraising domain to make sure both parents take part in as many of the duties as possible. With children, it is easy to imagine how the relationships at stake benefit from equal involvement in all aspects of their care; with housework, this "relationship" is less crucial on a day-to-day basis. That said, however, there is still magic in walking in each other's shoes by sharing as many tasks around the home as practically possible. Keep this in mind as you review some of the following ways you might handle sharing a given household chore.

Right down the middle. This is a real-time split, with each partner taking on half of a given task. In our house, we decided to split laundry this way after Amy noticed that she was washing all the clothes. After a quick discussion, we figured out why— Amy, like Catherine in her approach to dishwashing, has a much lower threshold for actually starting the washing machine; if the basket is full, it's time to do a load. Marc is content to let a few loads pile up and do them in a big batch (our joint definition of laundry covered what was included but left "how often" to individual preference). So we reaffirmed that laundry was something we wished to share—too big for either of us to be saddled with now and forevermore—and found a new way to do so. Now, Marc washes all the "darks" and Amy does the "lights." All family members sort the clothes they take off each day and place them in our two laundry baskets—one for each of us.

We like this way of dividing because it is so easy to manage. It is extremely clear that there is work to do when your own laundry basket runneth over, and yet we're free to go about washing our own fair share without waiting for each other. No one gets perpetually annoyed or feels guilty. Truth be told, division down the middle is pretty rare because not all chores lend themselves to this type of split. One ESP couple uses this division to handle yard work—he does all the planting, mowing, and raking in the front yard, and she takes care of the backyard. We think it works best for big, routine, endless but noncritical chores that you want to make sure are not unfairly dumped on either of you.

Almost exclusive. This method is far more common than down-the-middle division. Here, a task is primarily owned by one of you and dabbled in by the other—as determined by personal preference or level of vested interest. But what if one of you simply cares way more about *all* the housework than the other? This gets a bit tricky, but that's the beauty of setting joint standards before dividing the chores. Assign away, and give the obvious to the person who cares the most, but don't load this person up with a larger overall housework time commitment or far more essential tasks. We also encourage you to avoid deferring to gender stereotypes in all your decisions; you may end up with a typical gender division after all, but it is fine for most of the car maintenance to go to Mom and perfectly acceptable for Dad to do most of the grocery shopping. Finally, we challenge you to be flexible and mix up these assignments from time to time—even if just for fun. This avoids exclusive ownership of any chore by one partner, to meet the competency ideal of ESP. By steering clear of overt specialization—staying capable of pinch hitting for each other on any chore—you each remain fully appreciative of the other's efforts through empathy, you each have maximal freedom to walk out the door on a moment's notice without instructions, and you keep things fresh and interesting.

Many ESP couples use this method as their primary way of dividing chores. One dad handles the family finances and tracks the budget while his wife pays the bills. Another does the cooking and dishes while his wife commandeers the laundry ("Our crowning achievement is that we don't get bothered when one of us falls behind," this ESP mom tells us). In a reversal of traditional gender roles, another ESP mom does most of the lawn mowing, raking, and gardening, and her husband does more of the meal planning, groceries, and cooking. And another ESP husband, whose personal standards for household cleanliness are often higher than those of his wife, does more of the daily cleanup while she takes the lead on household projects. Pretty run-of-the-mill stuff. Almost exclusive chore division is probably closest to what happens in traditional families, only here the overall sharing of housework is equal instead.

Switch off. Alternating tasks back and forth or in a specific pattern is probably what most people think of when they hear about equally shared housework. Some critics have visions of a couple standing by the kitchen sink at night, each washing the same number of dishes. Or one person pausing before unloading the dishwasher to figure out if it's his or her night to do that. Despite these silly examples, switching off can be a useful and intimacy-building way to divide chores. It works best for tasks that have an established rhythm to them, or for chores tied to your work or home schedule.

Some examples of tasks ESP couples often share this way:

- Meal preparation (e.g., each parent is responsible for dinner three nights a week, with Friday as pizza night). One ESP couple alternates nights, allowing for take-out if the responsible spouse is too tired to cook—but the parent choosing this option is in charge of dinner again the next evening.

- Meal cleanup (e.g., rotate each night who cleans up while the other tends to the kids)

- Finances (e.g., one person handles the bills one year, the other takes over the next year)

This method of dividing tasks is the clearest way to walk in each other's shoes. You both get equal experience with each task and don't have to constantly negotiate whose turn it is to handle what. Yes, that means a bit of extra effort up front, but in short order the hand-off works almost unconsciously. And this method means you each get predictable breaks from any task. ESP couple Carl and Debby even used this method of task division as a means of globally sharing *all* tasks when their children were young, dividing up the week into twenty-one "shifts" of morning, afternoon, and evening, and each naming themselves responsible for ten shifts of housework and childcare duties (the remaining shift,

Saturday evening, was date night). Remember that in picking this option, you must choose the length of time between partner switches—a day, a week, a year, every time the chore presents itself, or some other time marking. And you have to avoid concerning yourself with when your partner is going to finish a task until it is actually encroaching on your turn.

As they come. With this option, responsibilities are shared without formal assignment. Instead, there is a rough operating system understood by both partners that says "whoever sees something that needs doing handles it as soon as time permits." This option is the most natural division because it flows from what is easiest for each partner to take on each day and is typically connected to how you both structure your time at home. It can work well for routine, obvious, essential tasks, like gassing up the car or buying the milk, but might not be as effective for more obscure tasks, such as filing your income taxes. As-they-come division is nice because it keeps you both observant and in the game every day, and can make you feel great about being mature, responsible partners. It does, however, require an especially high level of trust because the tasks are owned by the team rather than by one person. You may also need to occasionally check the equality; sometimes this approach to housework results in one person doing 90 percent of a chore you had planned to split more evenly.

All in the family. Here, both partners join forces to tackle a chore simultaneously. This chore "division" automatically creates equality and can mean a whole lot of fun and togetherness. Many ESP couples like to involve their kids in group cleaning projects, often setting aside a routine day of the week when all family members are expected to pitch in with the vacuuming and bathroom scrubbing. This can set a great example for the kids and take the pressure off any one person when the task is particularly thankless.

To each his or her own. This method means doing your own chores separately, and works well for tasks that you don't feel like comingling. In our house, for example, we do our own ironing as a general rule (surprise ironing gifts aside), which works out well because neither of us irons very often. This option is completely independent and not very intimacy producing, but it gets the job done. It isn't a good choice for chores that your partner or kids depend on; it would be a rather lonely household if everyone made his or her own dinner every night.

Outsource it. Finally, nothing takes care of figuring out who will do the mopping like hiring a housecleaning service, and nothing takes care of the autumn leaves like a lawn-care service. So, by all means, lay this option on the table for discussion when you can afford it. Of course, the more you outsource, the more you'll typically have to work to pay for your lifestyle. And the more you rely on others to run your home, the less connected you both will feel to this grounding domain. If maids and butlers buzzed around cooking every meal, stringing your Christmas lights, and planning your vacations, to use an extreme case, you would lose something intimate. That said, a little budgeted outsourcing can be a good thing—and can help you both save your precious time for your kids, yourselves, and each other.

Just as with joint task definitions, discussing how to divide or share a chore is necessary only if your division of labor isn't already working well. And although you may want to estimate how much time certain tasks tend to take each week in order to best share them, no complex formula is necessary to tell you when you've hit the magic goal of equal time spent overall by each of you on housework. A gut check is all that you need—easily done by asking yourself if you have a right to the complaint of "I do more." In fact, ESP couples specifically shy away from, as ESP mom Kitt calls it, "bean counting our chores" because we recognize this as "corrosive to our relationship"; while we are dedicated to equality, we prefer to step back and have deeper conversations about how we're sharing the care of our home rather than make sure the minutes spent on housework come out exactly even. Despite all the discussion in this chapter, the soul of ESP, in other words, is not focused too heavily on equal housework. Rather, it is about the courage to first become true partners and then treat each other as such every day. Equal chore division, in this case, is not so much the goal but the *result* of such a mentality.

So assign away—only as needed. Give your new arrangement a try for a few days or weeks. Keep the principles of ESP housework in mind as you tackle your own chores and observe your partner going about his or hers without criticizing. Renegotiate joint task definitions as needed. And most of all enjoy the team camaraderie and shared mission of a great relationship and a happy home.

Perks of Equal Housework

After a while, you may start to notice some interesting, perhaps unplanned, benefits of equally sharing the housework. We have experienced these, as have many of the ESP couples we've met, and chances are you'll feel them too. Here's a sneak peek:

Speed incentive. Once it is clear what's expected for a given task and who is responsible, each of you can develop comfortable routines to tackle your own jobs. The tasks have end points, whereas without clear boundaries and definitions, they can often feel like life sentences to the partner who is less inclined toward housework. This can lead to an incentive to zip through doing them. Once your part of the weekly vacuuming is checked off, it is done.

Reality housework. Forget reality TV—sharing the chores can give you a different kind of reality, the kind that keeps you both on your toes and in the action every day. One couple calls this "peak efficiency"—the feeling that two heads are better than one at optimizing how things get done around the house. Chores that would never be discussed in a traditional home are open for reen-gineering once they are fully shared, and both of you are moti-vated to trim time and effort, and learn from each other. This applies to purchases, too. Want a fancy new dryer? You can't get away with pretending you need it if the old one works perfectly fine, but neither can your spouse fail to understand if the old clunker just isn't cutting it any longer. Because you both know the details of how to run your home and why you run it the way you do, everything about housework can become more purposeful—more real.

More sex. Most of us want long-term, intimate, and sexually fulfilling relationships with our "other half." And recent survey data correlate a couple's frequency of sex with the fairness of their household labor division.[4] This is easy to understand. There is nothing sexier than a guy who has just capably cooked dinner, and then washed and put away your clean laundry. Well, maybe there are a few things sexier, but . . .

Equal sharing puts you on equal footing in your marriage, and this sets the scene for long-lasting intimacy. We strongly be-lieve that couples who are emotionally and mentally intimate are likely to be sexually intimate, too. At the end of the day (or first thing in the morning, or in the middle of the afternoon), you are lying next to your true partner—the person who knows how everything works at home, and who can and does do everything alongside you. How great is that? More than enough to get you in the mood.

That sounds lovely for the typical woman. But the typical man wins here, too. For him, ESP offers the likelihood that his

SHARING THE REMEMBERING

It is one thing to share all the household chores and quite another to share equally in remembering what needs to be done. This is the ultimate frontier of equal housekeeping and a concept that requires an advanced mastery of "minding your own business." Remembering is almost universally claimed by women. And as long as women keep handling the mental to-do lists and checking the calendar for upcoming appointments, bailing out their husbands time and again, nothing will change.

Changing this paradigm starts with giving your partner space to do the household remembering that occurs on his day at home, such as noticing that the diaper supply is nearing empty or that he's responsible for buying a birthday gift for Aunt Betsy's party tonight. If the baby needs changing and there are suddenly no diapers, let him handle it; chances are he'll come up with a spontaneous workaround that doesn't harm anyone. Aunt Betsy will probably survive if you attend her birthday party empty-handed, too, and your husband can be the one to apologize, if apologies are even necessary. Once it's clear you have stepped down from the home coordinator role, you can graduate to hard-core shared remembering based on your own assigned responsibilities. The day your husband says, "Honey, can you pick up more laundry soap when you're at the store today?" is the day you'll know you've crossed the border.

true partner is more attractive than a complaining, chore-bound wife. Nagging doesn't do much for attraction. Furthermore, some men think a woman who can handle the lawn care and build that patio is sexy, a woman who is not dead tired because she's done it all *again* is sexy, a woman who is able to bring home the bacon and fry it, too (just like him), is sexy.

Besides mutual appreciation and affection, the balance aspect of ESP can produce more *time* for sex. The two of you can make quick work of the evening chores after the kids are in bed, and then you're free to do as you please.

Everyday Execution

In this discussion, we've outlined an uncommon path to shared housework. Like anything rare, it can raise its share of doubts. It may seem artificial, for example, to first define what needs to be done—how it should be done and how often—and *then* divide the responsibilities. Of course, nothing ever works so neatly in real life! No one stops doing the cooking in order to tee it up for equality first. So instead of thinking about these two steps as a rigid approach to equal housework, we urge you to use them as your loose mental framework.

Let's say you're hosting a dinner party next week, and you'd both like to approach the preparation as equals. You might pause together and confirm what kind of party you want to throw. Then decide together on the type of food and entertainment—perhaps the budget, too—and jot down a quick to-do list with applicable deadlines; these are your joint task definitions for the party. Then you can divide up or share doing various items on your list and go about tackling your own duties without checking up on each other.

Some ESP couples are quite casual with their discussions of task definitions and assignments. Others are purposeful and specific—such as Cambridge, Massachusetts, ESP couple Dorea and Angela, both mathematicians who thrive on a systematic approach to life. They keep a notebook with a checklist of tasks to be done each morning and evening, including a weekly chore list outlining the schedule for less frequent duties, such as cleaning the bathroom and shopping for groceries. It also describes their concrete task assignments: Dorea prepares breakfast and packs lunches, Angela plans dinners and shops; they switch off who starts the washer in the morning and who dries and puts away the clothes in the evening; they're each charged with decluttering one main room (living room or bedroom) each day. The structure of their arrangement makes Dorea and Angela happy, and they enjoy spending time tweaking it to peak efficiency.

Some critics of equally shared housework point out how it involves such seemingly picky detailed communication—not just about creating joint task definitions but about dividing the tasks and staying equal over time. "It's only housework—why be so petty?" they say. This reasoning, we believe, is what got men and women into our collective mess of inequality in the first place. It is a bit like saying that stoplights at traffic intersections are trivial; details should not be confused with pettiness. By *not* having these discussions when they are needed, we risk confusion that sucks the life out of our relationships with power games, seething, nagging, and sarcasm—never mind marital crashes. ESP asks us to choose differently—to care enough about each other and our relationship to communicate and get in deep with the details when necessary, without being negative. Almost all ESP couples we've met truly enjoy working out these fine points with each other; they say things like "my wife/husband hears me" and "these are never onerous discussions."

A man who shares the housework participates fully in his home life—his home really is his own castle rather than a dwelling that functions by his partner's rules. A woman who shares the housework lives in a place of peace—her sanctuary rather than her demanding and lonely second job. By all means, if the home is running smoothly and everyone is happy, we're not here to ask you to stir things up. But if it isn't . . .

Home Tasks

What follows is a list of chores that may be candidates for joint task definition discussions. We've undoubtedly left off one or two, and probably include many you can cross off right away because they either don't apply or aren't contentious. Notice that the list contains some duties that aren't normally considered "housework," such as writing thank-you notes or handling one-time home improvement projects—but *everything* that goes into running the inside and outside of your home (except child-related or personal tasks) counts! Some chores may need to be broken into several smaller ones for discussion purposes (e.g., some ESP couples consider washing the laundry to be a separate task from folding or putting it away). You might use this list to create your own "hot button" chores, then share your personal idea of a job well done with your partner, listen to your partner's version, and negotiate the family's new definition:

Attending to family obligations (outside nuclear family)

Bathroom cleaning

Bill paying

Buying family presents (holidays/birthdays/other milestone celebrations)

Caring for ill/frail relatives

Car maintenance

Car washing

Clothes buying (nonchild)

Cooking

Dishwashing

Dusting

Entertaining (planning, preparation, hosting, cleanup)

Financial tracking/planning

Fix-it/home improvement projects

Gardening (planting, weeding, buying garden supplies, pruning, watering)

Getting gas for the car

Grocery shopping

Holiday decorating/planning/cooking

Home maintenance (chimney, gutters, etc.)—arranging or doing

Ironing

Laundry

Lawn mowing

Maintaining appliances/bicycles

Making decisions about the purchase of household objects

Meal planning

Organizing closets/basement/storage

Organizing the house (general)

Patio/deck care

Post office visits

Purging—donating/discarding items

Raking/bagging leaves

Shopping for household objects—furniture/décor items/ appliances

Shopping for household supplies

Snow shoveling

Taking care of dry cleaning

Taking out the trash/recycling

Tax preparation

Vacuuming

Window washing

Writing invitations/holiday cards

Writing thank-you notes

7

Self

IT'S ALL ABOUT YOU/YOU WITH A LIFE

If you're like most parents, it is only after you've taken care of the kids, logged your work hours, and finished the chores for the day that you allow yourself to think about doing something fun just for you. Personal time is not only the last thing you squeeze into your week; it's also usually the first to go when life becomes hectic. Yet a balanced life includes taking time for your own enjoyment. Taking care of yourself is what keeps you fueled to do everything else.

How well are parents doing at finding time for themselves? The answer is tricky because we're all so trained to sigh about our lack of time, and we're subtly judged (or so we assume) if we're spotted putting our own free time ahead of what we're supposed to do for others. Society rewards us for making sure our *children's* lives are filled to just the proper level with fun and enriching activities—for carting them off to science museums, playgrounds, puppet shows, mini-gymnastics, piano lessons, soccer, ballet, or children's story hour at the library. And we can usually remain exempt from criticism if our time gets eaten up all too often with long hours at work, travel to conferences, or working from home after the kids are in bed. Maybe if there's any time left over, we can score Brownie points by taking our spouses out on a date. But get out on the golf course alone or read a book "just because"—and do it routinely without shame? To most parents, that's crazy talk! So, the answer to the question of how well we're doing is either that we're seriously suffering from fun deficit or that we're amazingly good at pretending that's the case.

When we were expecting Maia, we knew that her arrival would change our lives forever. We understood that we'd each have to scale back our outside interests—we suspected this meant an end to movies whenever we wanted, reading a new novel every week, and frequent spontaneous dinners with friends. We were ready to cut back because we wanted to be with our baby most of all. But we loved spending time in these other ways, too, and felt anxious about those tales of new parents who all but disappear as individuals (tales really just about mothers, but we were committed to being equal parents). So we decided to be proactive. We promised ourselves that we'd hold on to at least one hobby each—hopefully more than one, but at *least* one no matter what. Marc chose tennis, and Amy chose playing the violin. By naming these two things aloud, we became less worried. Marc knew Amy's ears would perk up if he tried to schedule a tennis game or expressed interest in signing up for a tennis club during the winter; she'd be on board to make these happen. And Amy knew Marc would go out of his way to make sure she could get to string quartet sessions on Saturdays and to chamber music camp for a few days each summer. That taken care of, we were much better equipped mentally to scale back and could focus on the amazing news that our little girl was on her way.

In this chapter, we'll be exploring how to find time for the good things in life as a means to a balanced life in equal measure with your partner. In many ways, achieving *equality* in the self domain is a natural extension of equality in the other domains. It is the getting and protecting of this time—the carving out of this domain in *balance* with childraising, career, and housework—that is our biggest challenge.

Getting Personal . . . and Messy

What, exactly, belongs in the self domain? We think of it as holding all the things you do simply because you *want* to do them—other than routine time spent on the job, with the kids, or caring for your home. This definition casts a pretty wide net over purely fun adventures and hobbies as well as anything that is rewarding to you in any way. Spiritually restorative activities count, such as worship, community service, retreats, or a walk in the woods, as do physically nourishing ones, such as getting a massage, relishing a good meal, riding a bike, or climbing a mountain. Also included is time for social connection, such as getting together with friends.

Sometimes it can be a bit hard to judge whether a specific activity fits into this domain or not. There are those who think of washing the car as a chore, yet for others, it is a contemplative and peaceful activity. Many of us love working out at a gym—it is time to ourselves, helps us stay healthy and fit, and gives us that good high-energy feeling after we're done. Others dread this task and drag themselves through it just to check it off the to-do list. We might be called on to care for a sick spouse or friend, or our elderly parents—partly out of obligation but also with a deeper understanding that these actions bring us untold happiness in the long run. Are these examples of self time or self*less* time, spent on more than one's share of necessary chores?

This distinction is important. Recreation time is different for everyone, and only you know if an activity fits into this domain after you examine your personal motives for doing it. The key is to ask yourself (and pause to answer truthfully) why you're invested in spending your precious self time the way you do. If it's primarily for your own here-and-now enjoyment or personal fulfillment, you're in self-time mode. If it's for any other reason—your boss, your kids, your reputation, pure obligation, your neuroses—something else is going on.

We don't want to belabor this point—and risk sucking the fun out of thinking about your recreation time—except to add that we don't advocate trying too hard to tease this domain apart as a separate entity. And that means you might as well settle for "good enough" when you try to keep your personal time equal as a couple, giving up any attempts to tally your allotment with that of your spouse. It's not an exercise worthy of your time, so to speak.

No couple practicing any parenting lifestyle has ever told us that they want *less* time for fun. Even seasoned ESP couples with apparently balanced lives say that they have so many other things they want to do that can't fit into their days. But almost all proclaim that ESP gives each of them enough personal time to satisfy, that they're quite proud of their hobbies, and that they've taken active steps to keep them alive. They also commonly share that, like with our violin and tennis agreements, simply knowing

TRICKING OUR PARTNERS

t is easy to delude our partners into thinking we have no personal time at all by not owning our intentions. Take a scientist who slaves away in her cell biology laboratory searching for the cure for cancer, missing out on dinner with the family more often than not. While she may seem weary when she finally comes home after another long day, and even complain to her husband about how hard she works, she could actually be living her dreams. Or consider the compulsive homemaker who spends his extra time cleaning out the closets and organizing the drawers—well beyond what the couple has decided together is important to tackle. This extra career or housework time could actually be functioning as recreation time—voluntary time that energizes and fulfills—and these individuals' lives could be well balanced. Or not.

The truth matters to their partners. Our cell biologist may be the hardest-working woman in the neighborhood, but if her work hours keep her husband from his own time for fun week after week, they may want to reexamine what is going on. Our self-motivated home organizer may create beautiful closets and pristine drawers, but if this then leads to an expectation that his spouse similarly devote her time to such endeavors, a personal fulfillment imbalance could result.

they will each get time for their own interests makes it easier for them to handle stretches of time in any other domain. Their strategies are threefold: first, *take responsibility* for your own fun; second, *crush the guilt* that threatens your enjoyment; and third, *coordinate the time* with your partner.

Taking Responsibility

Long before Domenico, an ESP dad in Ticino, Switzerland, became a father, he discovered something important about himself.

He had spent many hours working hard in his IT engineering position, often traveling extensively for his job. But he slowly came to realize that work was not as important to him as he'd built his life to exemplify; he wanted a balanced life rich in other things, too. Most of all, Domenico wanted to paint.

So when he found himself laid off from work one year, he decided to take action on his dream and sent himself to art school for six months. He returned to a freelance offer from his former employer, which he negotiated to a four-day workweek so that he could continue to paint one day per week. Today, as a husband and father of two, Domenico has further reduced his work to three days—giving him a day each week to be home with his children while preserving his painting day.

Taking responsibility for your own personal life makes sense once you realize that only you know what makes you happy, and only you know when you're not getting enough of what does. It is not your partner's duty to figure out what fulfills you, spontaneously clear your calendar so you can do it, or even notice that you're not getting out much lately. These little chores are all your own. No magic formula can be applied to assess the adequacy of your personal time, but you can simply ask your gut to kindly tell you if it feels satisfied—knowing that you can't have fun, fun, fun all day long and that you wouldn't really want to anyway.

What have you done lately that is just for you? Are you able to take time to care for your health, get enough sleep, and keep at least one hobby or personal cause alive? Can you easily envision being able to carve out time for dinner or a movie with friends? Does your partner have similar freedom? You may not have all the time in the world to putter around the house, take up every sport that interests you, or head off to art school, but chances are you already know if your personal time is seriously out of balance.

So much to try, so little time! Because your goal is to create a balanced life with enough time for yourself—yet enough time for the other parts of your life, too—taking responsibility for your own fun means *prioritizing*. Signing up for a cake decorating class may mean you can't also join the women's bowling league without seriously jeopardizing your ability to get to your share of the household chores. If you decide to buy football season tickets, you may lose out on time to swim laps at the pool twice a week. ESP couples consider themselves grateful to have this problem of choice, and look upon the smorgasbord of options as an opportunity to be focused. In an ESP arrangement, you both know that the pool of free time is shared—that you only get half (but you do get half!). With this understanding, you're on the same team to optimize the available time. ESP couples also know that when one of you heads out for your adventure of choice, the other is often left to handle full parent duty—fully capably, we might add. But this is added stress nonetheless. Knowing all of this makes your choice of self time quite purposeful, but it can also heighten your enjoyment of that time.

Many ESP couples enjoy quiet activities in the evenings when the kids are asleep, such as knitting or reading, or short outings while they are in school, such as coffee dates with friends. Others take on pastimes that allow them to coordinate with their partners' schedulable hours away—singing in a choir or glee club, playing on a basketball or hockey league, going to monthly poker nights or book club meetings, or dedicating specific times to martial arts practice or running. Some involve their kids in their passions—not just the other way around—by taking them back-

packing or canoeing, joining together in activities at their syna-
gogue or church, or inviting them to participate in regular
at-home yoga sessions; as long as the child's presence is not considered an obligation, these parent-child activities often yield the
most enthusiastic discussions, since the parents get such a kick
out of the memories they are creating. Still other ESP parents
take on broad pursuits that they fit around their partners' schedules and their other obligations, such as the father who took up
semiprofessional photography, the mom who enjoys woodworking, the mom who started training for a half marathon as soon as
she finished breastfeeding her twins, or the dad who learned to
play the violin and now practices and performs regularly.

This chapter ends with a list of broad categories of recreational

FACING YOURSELF

A life without a lot of time for yourself means you can easily hide
behind your busyness. There is always someone else to attend to,
worry about, or pick up after. Then there's much-needed sleep when
you've finally finished each day of service to others. But if you actually
have time for reflection or pursuing a passion, you might be forced to
examine who you are before you can prioritize how best to use this
time. Are you interested in going back to school? Are you burning to
volunteer at a homeless shelter or on a political campaign? Are you
serious about getting better at windsurfing? All of a sudden, you're not
just someone's dad or mom, coworker, or spouse. But who are you?

This challenge is another gift of equally shared parenting or any
simplified lifestyle. It can be squandered by not taking your free time or
by using it for a few standard, safe-zone activities. Or it can be cherished as a way to learn new things about yourself, stretch your capaci-
ties, and become the wonderful person you know you are—completely
apart from your other everyday identities.

activities that can act as a launching pad for your own reflection and prioritization. You may already have a l-o-n-g list of unrequited passions waiting for that elusive "someday," but seeing the full scope of choices sometimes helps you decide where to start.

Crushing the Guilt

Has this ever happened to you? You get tickets to the NFL game on Sunday afternoon, and your wife bids you adieu with a smile. But that week you had to put in extra work hours to make a deadline, and you didn't see your kids nearly as much as usual. Your wife looks tired, and your kids were crying "Daddy, don't go!" when you left. You spend the first three-quarters of the game thinking about how you should be home, and then you leave before it ends. Or you negotiate time away to go shopping just for fun—a few hours in the big city or a trip to the outlets. The day comes and you awaken looking forward to your uninterrupted buying spree. You wave good-bye to your husband and your toddler, who have both come down with colds, and the guilt kicks in. You then spend the next few hours running madly between stores and making hasty purchases so that you can get home as quickly as possible.

Guilt has a way of messing up the whole point of recreation. Even if your partner shows no signs of trying to make you feel guilty, you can often do this job all by yourself. You can start to second-guess the importance of your time alone and figure it is just easier to stay home.

It is important to recognize that we are often our own worst enemies in the battle for personal time. Sometimes we just have to force ourselves out of the house when it is our turn to go.

Practice makes perfect, as they say. Hopefully, after we realize that the world didn't stop spinning because we took time to attend a play or meet friends for dinner, we can learn to let go of guilt. Maybe the best gift we can give to our families in return for our own time is to actually enjoy it and come home renewed.

Happily, ESP works against guilt specifically because of how it structures the rest of your life. The beauty of getting time for yourself is that you really aren't doing so at the expense of your children even if you had to work late a bit one week. This is because you've already built plenty of time with the kids into your standard schedule, and each child has an intimate and individual relationship with you (and their other parent). And when you leave them to go off on your own adventures, you are almost always leaving them in the capable hands of your spouse. While Mom is out at a movie with a friend, the children are getting bonus time with Dad. If she can then relax about her choice, she has a chance at real rejuvenation and fun.

An even stronger argument against guilt lies in what we're teaching our children by taking time for ourselves. No parents want their children to grow into stressed-out adults, but when we live this way, we are modeling it for them nonetheless. We are teaching them that children always come first; we are showing our kids that it is not very fun to grow up. The opposite option is to model joy. It may be even more important to show our kids how *we* enjoy playing the guitar than to teach *them* how to do so, because when we walk out the door to pursue a passion of our choosing, our actions can set the stage for our kids to pursue theirs.

But still, our culture has a way of making us feel irresponsible for sneaking out just for the pleasure of it. Any time we *could* be playing with our kids, working a bit harder, or finally getting to tackle those messy piles of paper—but instead we're doing something for ourselves—is still hard to rationalize. Especially if our chosen fun is not connected with some special occasion or mandatory for our health. And yes, it can be irresponsible if your partner is left holding down the fort every time you head out, getting nothing in return. But what if your Thursday night card game is matched by your spouse's Wednesday night volleyball practice? Then your guilt would lose its sting just a bit. In this respect, guilt is a barometer for *equality*. If your self time is in range with your partner's, you can look guilt in the face and laugh. If it isn't, guilt has a point.

Guilt can also be useful as a barometer of *balance*. ESP mom Jenn used to stay home with her three children while her husband worked long hours or was away on business trips. With this arrangement, she couldn't get past her guilt when she would contemplate leaving her husband to watch the kids so that she could have an evening out. "We had such limited time together once the kids were in bed, and I couldn't imagine cutting that back even further!" she explains. But now that this couple has converted to an ESP lifestyle, downsizing her husband's work hours and moving her back into the workforce, she reports, "The guilt is gone. We have plenty of time together now, so I can head out on occasion without feeling bad about it."

The more your life is nicely balanced among work, kids, home, and self, and your partner is enjoying a similarly balanced life, the less trouble you'll have batting down guilty feelings as you take time for yourself. In the end, guilt that warns us about imbalances and inequalities is helpful; guilt that comes from cultural expectations that we aren't supposed to prioritize our own enjoyment is not.

A FULFILLED PARTNER

Afamous saying goes something like: "Ain't nobody happy till Mama's happy." In this context, Mama rules the house. With ESP, both partners are equals, and it benefits everyone if both get time to themselves. A wife who is free to manage her own fun, and then does so, is a lot more fulfilled than one who feels trapped as a servant to everyone else's needs. A husband who can play without guilt is not likely to feel trapped in his life as a breadwinner, father, and spouse.

When we think of what makes a good marriage, things like communication, love, and respect come to mind. Marriage works best when partners nourish each other's dreams and help each other overcome barriers to make those dreams happen. Part of being a good husband or wife is giving your spouse the gift of time. Time for reflection, time to learn new things, time to tend to emotional and spiritual wounds, and time to take flight—these all contribute to being, and having, a healthy partner.

Goodwill is circular. If your partner believes that you want the best for him, chances are he will naturally want to give the best back. It can become as much fun to give as to receive. Watching your wife head out for a pedicure with a smile on her face may be just as enjoyable as going hiking yourself.

Coordinating Your Time

Once you're ready to take responsibility for getting a life, and you've stamped down any stray feelings of guilt, it's time to make your move—to negotiate your time away in an equitable manner. Compared to equalizing work, childraising, or household chores, this will be easy-peasy!

But where does the time come from in the first place? Most of us work hard, and many of us struggle to keep the house in manageable shape and the kids' basic needs met. The average set of parents would probably laugh at how "simple" it would be to divide up the remaining time between them—that's zero divided by two!

This is where the whole of ESP comes in—where we get to put our beliefs into action to create balanced lives rather than existences with no downtime. This isn't impossible to do if we want it badly enough! Here's a for-instance. Take your average stressed-out couple with kids and suddenly present them with a free trip for two to Hawaii—all expenses paid at the finest resort—with the condition that it must be redeemed by next week. Can you imagine how their minds would work overtime trying to make the needed arrangements to go? Somehow their coworkers would survive, their kids would be cared for, and their house wouldn't fall apart. This same miracle happens in emergencies, where seemingly impossible workloads can be put aside to care for someone in need. The idea with ESP is that you structure your lives somewhere short of all-obligation-all-the-time so that it neither takes an emergency nor a windfall to get you motivated to slow down and find self time. The time comes from all the purposeful decisions you've made about your career, your kids, and your housework already—balancing and equally sharing these domains with your spouse.

There are generally two types of time that you and your partner can turn into time for yourselves. We will call these *unrestricted time* and *negotiated time*. How you coordinate equal recreation time will depend on which type of time a specific activity requires. Unrestricted time consists of what's left of your nonworking hours after the kids are asleep (or otherwise without need of parental supervision) and the immediate household tasks have been completed. Naturally, each of you is free to pursue any activity during unrestricted time; you can choose to call a friend, surf the Internet, go to bed early, complete less time-sensitive household chores, log more hours for work, massage each other's feet, or organize your socks alphabetically by color. This type of time is assumed to be equal since your partner doesn't need to cover your absence. Well, technically, if one person wants to leave the house at night to attend a meeting of Toastmasters, then the other person is stuck at home; but beyond the physical barrier requiring one parent to be in the house with sleeping children, restrictions are negligible. One ESP mom, for example, goes for a nightly walk to clear her head once the kids are tucked in their beds.

Negotiated time is a whole different animal. Here, you're seeking to do something on your own during a time of day when parental childcare is required. This leaves your partner on duty at

STEALING TIME FROM TIME WASTERS

ESP doesn't manufacture time. But because you are dedicated to living a balanced life, it can help you redirect your time so that you feel like you have more. If you're like the average adult, you've probably spent many an evening plunked in front of the television passively absorbing whatever is on. This can be good for just relaxing and unwinding, but day after day of unimaginatively wasting time in this manner can be dulling instead of rejuvenating. By balancing work, housework, and childraising, you don't end all of your days harried and exhausted, and you can be more decisive about free time after the kids are in bed. Maybe you will still choose TV on occasion, but you could also decide it's time to cut the wood for those new shelves. Time for self is a funny thing; the less depleted you feel, the more you can be motivated to make sure it is rejuvenating.

home. Mom has to handle making dinner, giving baths, unwinding the kids before bed, reading the stories, and running up and down the stairs in response to "Mommy!" from their bedrooms—all while Dad is at the movies or at a buddy's house watching the big game. Or Dad gets the responsibility of handling every wail from a baby who wakes up five times nightly while Mom is roughing it far more serenely on that camping weekend with her sisters.

The actual arranging of negotiated time away requires mutual agreement. To get there, you'll need a few basic ground rules.

Rule 1: Respect the sharing. Getting time to do your own thing works best when your partner knows that *you* know this applies to *both* of you. Self time should be allocated such that neither of you feels shortchanged while saying yes over and over to the other's requests for freedom. If Dad wants to go to the gym after work three days per week and won't get home until 7:30 p.m., that's probably about five hours he's taking each week (and during the prime dinner hour, too!). He should be more than willing to free Mom for a leisurely get-together with a friend each weekend. Or if Mom wants to sleep in until 10 a.m. on a Saturday, it should go without saying that she can hold down the fort while Dad plays nine holes of golf sometime. Mutual respect—and a mutual understanding that self time is shared—fuels these arrangements.

Once you both feel your personal time is fairly shared, here are some ideas from ESP couples on how to *keep* things about equal:

- Beware of the planner/free-bird combination. If one of you meticulously plans out your leisure activities months in advance while the other prefers on-the-fly fun, the planner is essentially getting first dibs on the negotiated time. Just recognize this and try not to let it impede the more spontaneous partner's ability to get out.

- Choose carefully. Don't be afraid to "spend" your free time, but don't use it up on something that you know deep down is more obligatory than rewarding. Use ESP to give you the power to say no to unnecessary time commitments.

- Don't be petty about the exact hours owed you. Respect includes trusting that the time will even out—maybe not today, but next week or next month.

- Don't assume that your partner has to do your chores while you're away. Do them ahead of time or assume your tasks (other than immediately necessary ones) will be waiting for you upon your return. You may be pleasantly surprised, but you will not have taken your partner for granted.

Rule 2: Follow through. To make equal self time work, you both must commit to follow through with each other's plans except in the direst of circumstances. You should be able to count on each other when you make your plans to spend time on yourself. Mom's 7:00 p.m. book club meeting should not be automatically cast aside just because Dad wants to stay at work until 8:00 p.m. to finish a project. There is some degree of bucking up or working around obstacles required by each parent at one time or another.

ESP parents say:

- When you can't free your partner as scheduled, take responsibility for making alternative plans. Arrange for an appropriate babysitter, grandparent, or friend to watch the kids; take the kids with you; or help your partner reschedule his or her activity for an even better time slot.

- If you're the one missing out because your partner can't cover you for legitimate reasons, be understanding. As long as it isn't a pattern, graciously postpone your plans and move on.

- Be creative at scheduling, in order to minimize the chances your plans will be disrupted. Consider getting up early to run before your kids and spouse wake; playing hockey at 11:00 p.m., when ice time is available and your partner is surely home for the night; or getting your exercise during your daily commute by running or biking home on a set schedule.

Rule 3: Plan ahead. Within reason, both of you should give each other ample time to prepare for your absence so that the home parent can gear up for alone time with the kids (especially if it is all day or weekend). It is not reasonable, for example, to call your wife on your way home from work and announce out of the blue that you will be stopping at the local pub for the evening. She's been expecting you home at 6:00 p.m. and doesn't like to find out at 5:45 p.m. that she's on alone for baths and stories. Not that time with your kids is unpleasant, but when you have the mind-set that the duties will be shared at a given time, it is frustrating to have the game change so close to the end. This point becomes obvious once both parents are on solo-parenting duty an equal amount of time.

Here are some plan-ahead tips from ESP couples:

- Don't make any assumptions. It is not your exclusive prerogative to a block of time—clear it with your partner first.

- Don't close yourself off to last-minute opportunities either. Just take advantage of them in a spirit of equality by making unwelcome changes a rare thing, and assume your partner can do the same.

- Plan your recreation time around what works best for your family. You may find that next Wednesday is the best day to book your volunteer shift at the animal shelter, since your husband may have to work late on Thursday. One ESP couple purposefully tries to schedule their own evening personal activities for days when each has been "on" with their three-year-old son during the day; this way, they both get to see him for chunks of every day.

Rule 4: Don't prepare. One of the perks of ESP is that you don't have to instruct a clueless spouse as you leave him or her in charge of the home and kids to head out for any length of time. So, while it's a good thing to make sure your partner is aware of, and can cover, your planned absence, you should not stoop to preparing him or her in any other way. No need to precook meals to be eaten during your weekend in Vegas. Do not leave lists of things to do or reminders of when it is bath night. Do not call home just to check on things; call home to say "hello" and "I love you" and to share your adventures and hear all about theirs, but not to make sure the kids got their baths.

Here's what else ESP couples say about preparation:

- For ESP women: When you're out with others who marvel that your husband is handling the home front alone, or make fun of the fact that surely he isn't, don't play along. Just smile and let them know that he is at least as capable as you are.

- When you get home, don't walk around checking to see if everything was done to specification. Inquire how the time went while you were away, but only out of genuine interest.

- If you're the one staying home, take responsibility for planning the meals, picking up the milk if you're low, and setting up the activities/playdates/adventures that will occur while you're "on" with the kids. During extended spousal absences (e.g., multiple days or weeks), enjoy feeling like Superparent as you handle everything from nightmares to snowstorms to the sniffles—all by yourself. It feels great to know that you can do everything, and also that you've got a full partner coming home soon to resume the sharing.

Rule 5: No complaining. Nothing ruins a good time more than knowing your husband or wife is annoyed that you're having fun. Consequently, any attempt to make your partner feel bad for leaving you with the chores or with three cranky toddlers is forbidden. A stay-at-home parent is on single-parent duty all week, every week. A noninvolved father dreads having to handle all of the evening's activities alone so his wife can go out because he has not learned how to comfortably do them. ESP parents, however, escape both of these situations. This makes it more likely that an evening home alone with the kids and a mountain of laundry will actually turn into the best night of the week. Do not grumble— outwardly or inwardly—as your spouse heads out. Celebrate your partner's fun life and then make the best of yours.

ESP couples add:

- Don't complain to your kids either! Not that you would intentionally make them feel like burdens to you, but don't even complain about how busy or tired you are, or how you didn't get to go to your bridge club meeting last week.

- Relish the time alone with your kids. Make it special by going on a picnic for breakfast rather than staying home, baking cookies, painting a mural together with your bare feet, or just learning something new with them.

- When you return from your fun or relaxation, don't apologize to your kids. They enjoy seeing you happy! This makes their lives more secure. Instead, tell them about your experiences—what was important to you about your choice of activity, what you learned, how you felt, whom you met, and why it matters to you.

- Actively acknowledge your partner for being your ally in creating time for yourself by sharing your joy with him or her.

- Don't judge your partner's choice of free-time activity. Shared hobbies and interests are great, but even more important is shared enthusiasm for seeing each other happy.

COUPLE TIME

Since you married your true equal, you'll undoubtedly want to spend hours every week gazing into his or her eyes, no? While couple time doesn't require any classic negotiation for coverage, it can still be hard to come by when you're already balancing work, kids, home, and your own time for fun. But time together allows you both to connect through shared experiences that don't involve your children or your chores. In fact, most ESP couples put a premium on this time—as an extension of the intimacy that ESP provides to them in other ways.

Couple time may need to be borrowed from childraising, household chores, or work time in order to free you both up. Buying it through babysitters, childcare trades with other families, or extended family support, such as for a weekly or monthly "date night," may also be well worth the money. However, the biggest chunk of couple time that doesn't require a trip to the ATM or reducing your time with the kids comes in the evenings once they (at least the young ones) are asleep. We recognize that there are many philosophies out there for getting your kids to sleep. But there is very little disagreement that kids need sleep, and if you invest in good sleep schedules early and consistently, you get couple time every night for many years. Rent a movie, paint the bathroom, or share a candlelight dinner together. And, of course, there's always sex. It is good to know that some (or most!) evenings will be for the two of you together, rather than for each of you to go off in your own direction.

The Circle of Enjoyment

Time for yourself, or "me time," sounds so New Age. It is the subject of countless self-help books as well as the object of plenty of jokes. But deep down, almost everyone believes it is important to have space to catch your breath without being responsible for anyone else's needs. No one can sustain a life of giving without receiving. And we're not even speaking of selfish abandonment of one's children here. Rather, we're talking about preserving that part of us that is not defined as a parent, worker, or partner. We're something far more than any of these in spirit. Of course, taking up basket weaving doesn't define anyone either, but living a life that includes the possibility of weaving a basket comes closer to the ideal.

The beauty of personal time isn't so much that you get to sneak out to a movie once in a while or go to church on Sundays. Time for yourself is part of the full package of ESP—a balanced life with your equal partner. Once you are sharing time for meaningful careers, time for intimate relationships with your children, and time to care for your home, and once your own life is a balanced mix of each domain, sharing the rest of your time is only natural. And on the flip side, sharing recreation time can lead to more equal sharing in the other domains. Maybe today you agree to cover your wife for a weekly pottery class. Later, when you find that she comes home beaming with her clay creation and you had a blast during that evening alone with the kids, you both might be ready for a bigger step. Sooner than you think, you'll be downsizing your job to have more time with your terrific children, and she'll be accepting an equivalent job as a potter. You never know!

ESP couples often express to us that a side benefit of enough time for themselves is that they can fully enjoy time together as a whole family. Because neither parent is depleted at the end of the workweek, these couples often have the energy and desire to head off for Saturday adventures with kids in tow—and often choose to do this over taking more time for themselves or as a couple. "Date night out is not that exciting to us," says Helena. "We see plenty of each other every evening at home as it is. Give us some extra time, and we'll spend it hiking with the kids, or save it for an occasional three-day weekend getaway instead."

No matter how you structure your self domain, ESP gives you the courage to hold on to your own identity amid all the responsibilities for your job, your loved ones, and your home. Yes—you deserve this time. Yes—your kids deserve to see you happy and fulfilled, doing what you believe in with your own time. Yes—your spouse deserves the best of you, which is possible when you can take care of yourself mentally, physically, emotionally, and spiritually. Once you can get past misplaced guilt, you are on your way. Finding ways to use this extra breathing room, and to enjoy watching your partner do the same, is all part of the fun of having time for yourself. You each have a life that suits you, and one that reflects joy back onto your family.

Self Activities

What follows is a list of some categories of activities you might consider enjoyable or renewing. We invite you to use this list to consider how you currently spend your time and whether you'd rather spend it elsewhere. You can also talk with your partner about his or her personal time choices and ask yourselves if you feel either of you gets more or less time than the other to do what you want.

Adventures

Blogging

Classes (generally not career related)

Dining

Exercise

Games—board/cards/computer/other

Hobbies

Internet surfing

Meditation and spirituality

Music—participating/observing

Organizational activities (nonwork)

Personal projects

Physical health (doctor, dentist, acupuncture, massage, etc.)

Reading

Relaxation (general)

Religious-affiliated activities

Retreats/spas

Salon services

Self-help—group meetings/therapy sessions/conferences/
journaling

Social activities/events

Sports—participating/observing

TV

Vacations

Volunteer activities or philanthropy

PART THREE

NAVIGATING THE BARRIERS

very parenting relationship is unique and complex. But when you build yours on principles rather different from what is customary, you add a new layer of intricacy: two equally valuable careers combined with equal parenting responsibilities, jointly shared housework, and equivalent opportunity for personal time—and a balanced life for both of you. When most of the couples around you aren't reaching for these particular stars, the road can get rather lonely and doubts can creep in about the wisdom of your decisions. Worse yet, the rest of the world can often seem downright uncooperative when it comes to honoring your choices—such as arranging your work and childcare so that you can stay equally involved in all of life's domains. When circumstances get rough, the strength of your belief in equality and balance will be tested.

The two most common barriers to creating and keeping an ESP life are financial considerations *and* cultural expectations. *After reading through this book so far, you may be wondering how you could possibly make such an arrangement work with your expenses. Or you may be concerned about how an ESP life would play out in your own workplace, neighborhood, schoolyard, and circle of friends. The next two chapters will help you gather the tools to dismantle these barriers.*

Money

YOU HAVE ENOUGH/SPEND IT WISELY

"Gee, must be nice, but we could *never* afford that." This is the response we get over and over from so many traditional or dual-income couples after they hear about equally shared parenting. Without even a minute of contemplation, these couples rule out a life of equality and balance because they think it is too expensive. They get one whiff of the part-time work that many ESP couples have arranged, or even the full-time but flexible careers that others carry, and erect a knee-jerk barrier to claiming such a life for their own. How sad!

True, very few of us can escape the reality that money fuels our daily lives—we need to make it and we need to spend it to pay for our routine expenses, save it for the future, and once in a while fritter it away on an ice cream cone. While a few of us have all the money to cover our every need and desire, most of us feel as if we're just getting by and worry about falling into debt with a slight twist of fate. But the mental leap to assume that ESP means sacrificing financial solvency simply makes for a great excuse not to explore a new way of life. It just doesn't have to be true.

In this chapter, we'll wrestle down the money barrier and show you what really happens in the lives of couples who veer off the "safe" path of earning and spending as a way to create the relationships they want—here and now. We'll examine the financial impact of this decision, focusing first on how money is earned and then on how it is spent. Along the way, we'll show you that, contrary to popular opinion, ESP is often cost-neutral and can actually *save* money for some couples—all while offering a host of other priceless rewards.

In previous chapters, you've been introduced to some couples who have made unusual career decisions to achieve ESP. Some have made giant leaps away from consumerism and their formerly high-earning lives. But many others have made far less drastic changes. So don't worry! We aren't plotting to turn you into fringe members of your community—that oddball family that no one sees and that is rumored to live off visits to the town dump. We won't be asking you to trade in a surgeon's salary for the wages of a lumberjack either. ESP couples live quite happily amid mainstream society. But we are among the many who have made a decision to question the ins and outs of money and to decide for ourselves how we'll use it. Specifically, we aim to use money to *further our balance and equality* rather than to put them at risk.

There is nothing about living as equal partners that requires any particular level of wealth—even the poorest couple is capable of sharing the cooking and the diapering. We'll also show you that lower-income couples are fully able to achieve balanced lives, although families living in abject poverty clearly find every day difficult regardless of their chosen parenting arrangement. In fact, we suspect (without any real data to back up our suspicions) that ESP may be more difficult for the very *rich* than for us common folk; many wealthy couples tend to build their financial power on the success of one partner, and that partner can fuse his or her identity to this success so strongly that ESP becomes mentally unreachable. We've all heard the stories of former Fortune 500 CEOs who have chucked it all for the simple life, but the typical top-of-the-world corporate tycoon is probably the least likely person to remake himself into an equal partner with a balanced life— and not because he doesn't have the money, ability, or power to do so! It's true that pioneer ESP couples are typically middle-class professionals with college educations or beyond—but not always.

Earning Money

Mary Ellen, a nurse, and Ariel, a housepainter, live in Olympia, Washington, and share in raising their four children, ranging in age from four to seven. They have arranged their work schedules so that, in alternating fashion, one of them is home with the kids every Friday, and set up their work shifts so that Mary Ellen drops the children off at school before heading in to work and Ariel is home most days when they get home. In the evenings, they both pitch in to help with the cooking and the kids' homework, and on weekends they make family projects out of the laundry and housework.

Mary Ellen and Ariel tell us that neither feels burdened, and they consider themselves lucky to have so much family time. They feel especially grateful to have learned the lessons of a diversified income to help them ride the waves of a fluctuating economy. "We have the security that either of us could ramp up our income if necessary," says Mary Ellen. "If I'd opted to be a stay-at-home mom, I wouldn't have the work experience to do that so quickly." At a time when most couples would consider increasing their *income* to pay for such a big family, this couple chose instead to optimize *time* with their kids in a way that gave them enough money to live comfortably and the security that they could make income changes as necessary.

Ariel and Mary Ellen's lives illustrate several common ESP approaches to earning money. In particular, they showcase the three rules of ESP earning: *Do the math* so that you can gauge the true cost (or surprisingly, savings) of ESP, *leverage your risk advantage* of two moderate careers to reach more financial security, and *know when you have enough money* so that you can trade it for more time. Let's take a look at each of these concepts.

Do the Math

We wonder what would have happened if this book had been titled something like *Getting Rich with Equally Shared Parenting*. Would a whole new subset of parents be drawn to thumb through its pages? Although we don't think of ESP foremost as a wealth management strategy, this cheesy, suck-'em-in title (with its double meaning) would not have been far from the truth for many couples!

It is common to assume that regular two-income families have the best revenue stream and that a family with one stay-at-home parent is making a significant financial sacrifice to swing this arrangement. But with ESP, you've got a hybrid that requires a bit more analysis. Here, both parents remain in the workforce in either flexible full-time jobs or reduced-hours positions. Both are motivated to be artisanal workers, who do their best on the job each day and tend their career paths over time. They may not earn exactly the same amount of money, and neither of them can elect to plow past the other to a more "important" position that might maximize individual earnings (and force the other to make large career compromises), but both are fully capable of providing their share to the family bank account. Because they've cut back their work hours or altered their work schedules to create balanced lives, their net outside childcare needs are often considerably less than those of a non-ESP dual-income family (all the way down to none in many cases). We sometimes think of an ESP couple as sharing the childraising time of a stay-at-home parent between them, and yet they usually earn a combined salary that far surpasses that of a single-breadwinner family.

Every family work option garners a specific amount of money, which depends heavily on the individual salary and earning power of each parent, the cost of commuting, outside childcare, and other variables. If you set aside all the expenses that don't immediately vary with work arrangement options, such as your mortgage payment, you can begin to decipher the basic net income of any given scenario for your own family. This personal analysis is crucial and so often glossed over with ready-made assumptions by all those couples who say ESP is not affordable. Therefore, the First Rule of ESP earning is to *do the math*!

Don't make it a big production. Just grab a calculator and gather a few basic figures. Add up how much you currently earn together and how much you pay today for outside childcare (or that you estimate you'll pay if you are not yet parents or are still on parental leave) to get a rough idea of your net income. Then, brainstorm wacky ideas for other ways both of you could piece together your work schedules, jobs, commutes, and so on. Think about how each of these ideas would impact your child-care costs and the number of hours your kids will spend in outside care. Ask other parents about their childcare options—costs, schedules, availability—and consider what would happen if you swapped all or part of your current plan with any of these ideas. Estimate the net cost of all sorts of possibilities. The goal here is to get everything out into the open and to either alleviate or confirm the financial concerns you may have around building the work/home schedules you want and the lives you want for your children.

How much would it cost your family if you worked only four days per week and your partner ramped up (or down) to four workdays, too? What would happen if you worked from home every Tuesday? What about simply cutting out overtime or shifting your start time by one hour? How would *any* work change affect your weekly childcare expenses, your commuting costs, your tax bracket, your healthcare benefits, your retirement or college savings? Warning: If you're dead set against the possibility that ESP could mesh well with your family finances, you will be able to find a way to support this view in your calculations. However, just like crunching the numbers to find out if you can afford a new car or a trip to Antigua, you could find out that ESP is fully

MATH IN ACTION

et's look at how "doing the math" might work out for an example couple—one in which Dad and Mom currently work full-time and require forty hours of outside care for each of their two preschool children (eighty hours total). Let's say grandparents aren't readily available to provide this care for free, so they've enrolled their children in a daycare center. Dad currently grosses about $60,000 annually, and Mom brings in about $40,000. Childcare costs them $7 per hour for each child, which means $560 weekly or about $28,000 per year. It's abundantly clear why this family might traditionally choose to keep Mom home based on finances. After taxes and ancillary work expenses, her salary just barely covers daycare costs.

However, if both parents were able to compress their workweek into four 10-hour days and stagger their schedules a bit, they could reduce their daycare bill by 40 percent (to three 8-hour days). That's a savings of $11,000 annually, which is closer to $15,000, since most daycare is paid with after-tax money. Not to mention the added benefits of keeping both parents plugged into their careers and their home life, and giving each of them a full day with their children. In this example, ESP actually nets this couple over $10,000 to their current bottom line. That's like the family getting a 10 percent raise!

Let's extend this theoretical example by assuming that both parents could also reduce their work obligations by 20 percent, working four 8-hour days instead. If they also staggered their schedules, their daycare requirements could be further reduced, maybe enough to cover much of the $20,000 in reduced income. And they'd have the best shot at balanced lives. What may have initially seemed impractical now has financial appeal. For a relatively small net monetary impact on the family, these parents might find themselves with time for recreational activities, stress-free running of errands, or even sleeping an extra hour.

Dreaming about the possibilities and crunching a few numbers can be a great motivator to creating the life you want.

within your financial grasp. What would it cost, or perhaps even save, to have the life you want?

Check out the Toolbox section on our website (www.equally sharedparenting.com) for an online worksheet that can help you do some of these quick calculations, or get fancy with your own spreadsheets if you wish to delve into more of the details.

Notice that these calculations yield the most savings from the ESP model for families at *lower* income ranges; relatively wealthy couples may not appreciate the reduced childcare costs that accompany many ESP arrangements, whereas poorer families will save a much higher percentage of their income with each hour of outside childcare saved (unless they have highly subsidized or free childcare). Note, also, that the math is most dramatic for couples with high childcare bills, such as those with children under the age of five. Every family's situation, of course, is unique—which is why it is so important for you to set your own goals and then do your own math. Run your numbers, think about the income consequences of all sorts of tweaks to your current work schedules, and have fun narrowing in on what fits best for your family.

Leverage Your Risk Advantage

In a traditional family, one partner is often considerably more responsible than the other for bringing in the money. One spouse either is the sole source of income or has been designated as the main breadwinner with the career and salary that count. The danger here is that this person could be laid off or injured in a way that topples this arrangement and can threaten the family's financial (and emotional) well-being. Such a couple could send the nonworking or just-dabbling-in-work spouse out into the workforce in earnest if necessary, but it may not be so easy to suddenly make this happen. The dual-income couple avoids this danger, or so one might think. But many non-ESP dual-income couples are at as much (or more) risk of bankruptcy because they have come to rely on the full amount of both salaries.[5] They've used their combined income to buy their way into top-rated communities with highly touted school systems, or to secure a mortgage for a bigger house. Or they have simply let cultural influences and advertising work on their purchase decisions because they have the disposable income to spend. Now they have nowhere to move if one of them becomes unable to work. Both of these standard parenting arrangements are prone to financial instability.

An ESP arrangement brings its own worries ("How long will I be able to keep this fantastic flexible job?" "What if my wife's boss insists she travel on Thursdays, her day home with the kids?"), but many ESP couples escape the bulk of the big fears of standard family breadwinning. If one parent in a couple with two part-time workers is unable to work, the other can return to a regular full-time job with relative ease; both have maintained meaningful careers and kept up in their fields so as to command a full-time salary if necessary. And yet the family has had to make do on the income of two ESP parents—typically less than the combined gross income of two non-ESP dual-earner professionals (childcare costs notwithstanding). If they aren't poor money managers, they have already limited their spending to meet this reduced income, and ramping up the other partner's earnings can often tide them over quite nicely (while the out-of-work spouse can competently take up the childraising hours temporarily relinquished by the spouse increasing his or her work hours). An ESP family also typically loses a smaller percentage of its total income if one partner is out of work than if the primary or sole breadwinner or one of the dual earners is laid off.

The financial confidence that comes from having two active yet moderate careers can also be used to an ESP couple's advantage in happier times—not just during layoffs. Specifically, each parent has the ability to play around with his or her career path in order to optimize some aspect of a balanced life—and rely on the other partner to hold up the family finances in the meantime. Both partners get this benefit, not just one, which maintains their equality. Maybe a computer programmer dad dreams of leaving his corporate, no-patience-for-family-concerns boss and taking another job with a more sympathetic supervisor or becoming self-employed so he can control his own hours. Perhaps a lawyer mom wants to return to school to train for a more flexible career in public health (or graphic arts, for that matter). These are bold moves—not unheard of, but often made easier by the safety net of ESP.

We've heard time and again from ESP couples that their commitment to sharing gives them the courage to finance their dreams. Take Windsor, Ontario, couple Jenn and Aaron, for example. Jenn became a stay-at-home mother when their first child was born, and Aaron worked long hours as a mechanical engineer; they continued this arrangement for over six years as they welcomed two more children. But deep in Aaron's heart, he knew he wasn't where he wanted to be. He grew up watching his firefighter father, and more than anything wanted to follow his path. He also acutely felt the loss of time with his children. It took Aaron five years and three lengthy application processes to land a paying position as a firefighter, and the family absorbed a carefully budgeted 50 percent cut in his pay. Jenn also reentered the workplace to fund Aaron's dream; she took a job at Starbucks for about twenty-five hours per week, grateful for a position that allowed her to fit her work hours around Aaron's rotating schedule of two 24-hour weekly shifts. And what about Jenn's career? Her turn to benefit from the risk-taking ability of ESP has now arrived; she has had her eye on a midwifery training program (a career that also lends itself to fitting with Aaron's) for a while, and has just left Starbucks to work as a doula. Says Jenn: "The births happen in their own time, but the prenatal-postnatal visits get scheduled around our family's schedule for the week. I am currently only taking two births per month in order to keep a healthy balance. This may change as I get a better hang of managing how this works, or it may not. We both have jobs we are passionate about now."

In this example, one spouse reentering the workforce made it possible for the other to pursue a lower-paying but more satisfying career. In other ESP families, one partner's current job acts as a life preserver for the family's needs while the other partner looks for a job with more flexibility or a shorter commute, or starts his or her own business. One couple used the security of two moderate careers to give them the courage to move from a big city with plenty of job opportunities to a small resort town. "We would never have moved here if we had to depend on only one job," says this ESP mom. "But with two jobs, we have little worry about providing for our family. We can survive on one eighty-percent salary, and knowing that lowers our stress level tremendously."

This security holds true for the nonmonetary aspects of job

changes as well. *Any* couple with two substantive sources of income might be able to handle a temporary job loss or change in one spouse's career from a monetary perspective, but the homecoming of a previously working parent can have significant ripple effects for the family's daily life. With an ESP family, however, fewer adjustments to outside childcare are often needed, and less change typically happens in the life of the family. Using us as an example, Marc's layoff brought him home only three additional days each week; this wasn't enough to bother downsizing our outside childcare hours (which were far less than full-time to start with) while he spent that time looking for work. The only thing our kids noticed was that Daddy, who was already fully competent at childraising and housework, was perhaps home a bit more in the mornings and late afternoons on those three days.

The Second Rule of ESP earning, therefore, is to *leverage its risk advantage.* It's like redoing that old saying about the rich getting richer: the balanced get even more balanced!

Know When You Have Enough Money

Judy and Bruce in Providence, Rhode Island, are about as dedicated an ESP couple as you'll ever meet. Judy is a former lawyer who runs a consulting and training practice around diversity in the workplace three days per week, and Bruce is a family doctor in a group practice who has reduced his workload to 80 percent (three weekdays plus periodic on-call and weekend obligations) since the first of their three children was born. For Judy and Bruce, ESP was an outgrowth both of feminism and a joint desire to limit the daycare needs of their children as infants. But once they both secured reduced-hour arrangements, they were hell-bent on never turning back. "What a great idea it is to work only three days a week!" exclaims Bruce. "My boss mistakenly assumed I'd return to a full load a few months into the change, and kept asking me if I was ready to come back full-time. My answer was always 'No way!'" Bruce absolutely loved his time with his children; he loved being the trailblazer dad on the playground; he loved making up all sorts of silly and endearing games and adventures on his Daddy Days; he couldn't believe other fathers would ever pass up this opportunity. *Oh wow, it's Tuesday (or Friday),* he'd think. *I get to hang out with my kids!*

Their firstborn now off to college, Judy and Bruce are on the "launching" end of their parenting life and like to look back at what has happened, what might have been, and how they feel about it all. In their emphatic way, they say they wouldn't change a thing. As odd as it seems for a lawyer and a physician to say, they tell us that they figured out something valuable early on— that neither of them had aspirations of climbing higher. Judy settled happily for a lower-paying career, and Bruce became a terrific doctor who brought home 80 percent of the relatively lower physician's salary associated with a managed-care practice. Like so many ESP couples, they chose time over money.

Judy and Bruce's story exemplifies the Third Rule of ESP earning: *know when you have enough money.* We've already touched on the idea of buying time in Chapter 5, but here we want to emphasize that it is possible to actually calculate (or estimate) how much money you need and make concrete decisions not to gun for more. ESP couples tell us that they don't miss any of the money they could have earned. In their moderate careers, especially if they choose relatively high-earning ones, they have plenty. Yet it is so common for us to want more—to think we need more.

In Chapter 5, we advised you to work toward a high pay rate per hour as an artisanal worker, and then to use your hourly pay to consider working less rather than earning more. Here, we're recommending that you also drop your future earning power worries. Could you bring in more money working for decades in some other career or at a different job? We imagine so. You would likely end up with more funds for retirement or for your children's educations with some peak-earnings career, or perhaps money for many more possessions or exotic trips for your family. There is no limit to the amount of money any of us can find uses for, and almost no amount at which we will no longer have to worry about affording anything. Where do we draw the line, then? Would the extra money really bring you, your partner, or your children more happiness? To borrow a line from Bruce, "No way!"

Spending Money

Let's turn now to the other side of the ledger: the money that goes out. We buy a lot of stuff with our money, from our basic shelter to insurance policies to the most frivolous of doodads. We spend it giving gifts to others, supporting charities near and dear, keeping up our health, and keeping up with the latest trends. We have fixed expenses, such as a car payment or our kids' private school tuition, and variable expenses, such as how much we shelled out this week on lattes or library late-book fines. You've probably read horror stories about the level of debt an average American family lives under (or perhaps you know firsthand).

Earning more is not the only way to solve the financial puzzle. In addition to becoming conscious of how much money we bring in, ESP helps us become clear about how we want to spend it—which is, of course, a terrific idea for anyone! The three rules of an ESP *spending* mind-set are: *track your expenses, live below your means,* and *spend consciously.* Let us elaborate . . .

Track Your Expenses

Money is one of the least transparent things in life. We may know gobs of intimate details about our friends, but chances are we have no idea what's in their bank accounts—whether they are wealthy, teetering on bankruptcy, or humming along with just enough—even though we can see much of what they buy and can make decent guesses at their salaries. Their spending habits, in particular, can belie their actual finances; they could be socking away tens of thousands for future use or going slowly into debt even as they buy a new car every three years or head off to Paris for a romantic weekend. You just never know.

This not knowing can play tricks on our priorities, because even if we purposefully set out to avoid keeping up with the Joneses, most of us still want to fit in where we live, work, and play. So we end up adjusting our spending to mesh at least amicably with those close to us—often without much thought to what we're doing. We may feel obliged, for example, to pay the fee for that neat-o after-school science class because our kids' friends are all signing up or because, well, it's there for the taking. Or follow the lead of millions and take the kids on that "required" trip to our culture's Mecca—Disneyworld. Or buy a riding lawn mower or own multiple cars just because it is so easy to assume that these standards are necessities in our particular neighborhood.

The pressure to spend money the way our social circle says it should be spent is underappreciated by most of us. It is enormous. Then heap on the power of advertising from our market-driven business culture, and pretty soon we're spending for external reasons rather than based on our own values. Our money is managing us rather than the other way around, all because it is nearly impossible to be honest or open about money. The ESP life doesn't align well with all this secrecy, however. Making purchase decisions without a full understanding of where our money goes works against creating the balanced life and equal partnership that we seek. Therefore, the First Rule of ESP spending is to *track your expenses*.

Groan. Unless you're an accountant, the idea of keeping track of everything you buy probably sounds deeply unpleasant. Yet you undoubtedly know the value of doing so, and if you've forgotten, please allow us to remind you. When you know how much money your family spends, on average, buying groceries every month, you can begin to determine if that's how much money you *want* your family spending on groceries. If you suspect your partner is spending an inordinate amount of money on shoes, you can check your assumptions (you might come to find that your sports receipts dwarf your beloved's footwear indiscretions). If you want to buy a new bedroom set this year, you can figure out easily if you can afford it—by looking at your current level of income and spending. These obvious benefits will be addressed in the next sections of this chapter, but they are all made possible through a good understanding of what you are buying.

The idea we want to convey is that knowledge is power and ignorance is limiting. So if you haven't already done so, please invest the time (and a minimal amount of money) to get a tracking system in place. We use a software program to do so, but choose whatever method is most useful to you, including paper and pencil if you wish. Set up some spending categories (e.g., dining out, groceries, clothes for him, clothes for her, clothes for each child, books/magazines, each utility, car payments, mortgage/rent, household goods, dry cleaning, pet supplies/health, medical, dental, and gas) and simply begin to categorize and enter each of your purchases. Credit cards, by the way, can streamline your expense tracking through downloadable reports of all your purchases; they aren't as evil as some money gurus paint them to be—as long as you always pay off the full balance at each bill. Then, run a report each month or so (or whenever it interests you) to check on your spending habits. After a few months to a year of doing this, you'll have a great picture of what happens to your paychecks—and will likely be less tempted to unconsciously imitate how the neighbors seem to be spending theirs.

Live Below Your Means

As we meet ESP couples and talk with them about their lives, we are struck by the fact that many seem to prioritize living below their means. Some of them make good money and simply spend a bit less than they make. But others consider themselves part of a simple living movement and perk up whenever we ask them how they've learned to spend less. Living below your means is just plain common sense, of course, but it takes a certain "no thanks" attitude toward those social pressures and business marketers to actually pull it off.

Once you've lifted the confusion from what you spend— thanks to your expense tracking—a quick comparison to your income can easily tell you if you're accruing money over time or if you're slowly sinking into debt. This is an important assessment

CONSUMER BEWARE!

We'd be willing to bet that you have no idea how many advertisements flicker past your eyes every day. A conservative number is almost 250, and our children's naïve eyes typically take in 25,000 advertisements annually from television alone.[6] Companies want to sell their stuff, and we are the means to that end. But sadly, businesses don't stop at blatant commercials; they aim to create a culture in which you begin to think you'd be a fool not to buy their products. Fashions change each season—hmmm . . . Fast-food chains sell unhealthy meals using kid-friendly cartoon characters and free toys (toys often tied to movies rated PG-13, by the way) so that our children become lifelong consumers who equate their products with the comforts of childhood. New versions of software are released each year with marginal improvements. (Marc knows all about this in his line of work.) And the newest prescription drugs are touted to the public as miracle cures, even though older generic drugs often work just as effectively and safely for a fraction of the cost. (Amy's seen plenty of this at her job.) In every industry, there are legitimate but cunning ways to get us to buy what we don't need.

Doesn't this make you even a little mad? Marketing creates need, invents diseases, bullies and belittles those without the latest "stuff," and generally messes with our minds. We don't want to bring the capitalist economy to a screeching halt, but we can begin, slowly, to understand that we can either be taken or take back our power. Let's go for empowerment.

to check on periodically, so that you have a fighting chance of living below your means. And living below your means is your ticket to freedom from worry.

Let's take a look at how two ESP couples approached living on less than they earn. In fact, we'll ask the same two couples we profiled in Chapter 3 on sustainability to be our spokespeople once again: Pete and Simi, and Melissa and Richard. If you recall, Pete and Simi traded in their software engineer positions for self-made careers in carpentry and financial management; they each typically work less than fifteen hours per week and share in the care of their four-year-old son. And Melissa and Richard reduced their work hours to twenty to thirty weekly, completely eliminating the need for outside care for their two daughters by staggering their workdays. Remember that reduced-hour work is not a requirement for ESP; the fact that it is financially feasible, however, makes these two examples useful to explore.

How did they each accomplish this financially? Melissa and Richard are clear about how: by having children well after establishing themselves in their careers and by shaving off the expenses that don't matter much to them. Their lives are wholly mainstream; they live in a single-family suburban home near Boston. Their daughters attend a private elementary school, and they travel to Europe each year to visit relatives.

But Melissa and Richard have built solid careers that net reasonable paychecks, and they carefully make sure that those paychecks cover all their expenses. Limiting their personal spending involves simple strategies like having only one (old) car, no television, and no magazine or newspaper subscriptions. Lunches are made, not bought, and their coffee is brewed only at home. Public transportation is commonly used. Internet connectivity and a cellular phone come courtesy of Melissa's job, as she works from home a small part of the week. To increase family time and save money in the process, they skip the aftercare programs at their daughters' school. A family activity for Melissa, Richard, and the girls is a walk in the woods rather than a spree to an amusement park; they visit a mall only about twice every year, and never for recreational shopping. And as Melissa is fond of saying, "We just love to use things up." In our throwaway culture, this couple doesn't automatically replace their old stuff with new versions, or find the need to get the most elaborate or fanciest type of anything. Melissa and Richard also credit their high level of organization with keeping them on track financially.

Rather than feel like a sacrifice to Melissa and Richard, their frugality has become somewhat of a mission—they both like what they are teaching their children about money and earth-friendly living, and they feel it helps them stay family-centered. Melissa and Richard say they would live this way even "if we were zillionaires," but since they aren't, it also feels like a gift that keeps financial anxiety at bay.

Pete and Simi, on the other hand, embraced living *far* below their means early in their careers and now reap the benefits of early investing. Their plans were based on the idea that if they stopped spending excess money, they could control their own lives—how much they would work, where they would live, what they would do for work, when they'd be able to take off on adventures. Their first move was simply to focus on saving money—to experiment with setting aside larger and larger portions of their full-time salaries.

As the ball got rolling on their ratcheted-down spending, their excitement grew. Each item not purchased was a victory. Everywhere they looked, they began to see useless ways to spend their money, and as time ticked on, their bank accounts grew. Careful accounting and secure investments for their money (including the purchase of rental property) gave them the courage to quit their jobs and start their "early retirement" careers about four years after they first embraced their savings plan. Still, they figured that the huge drop in income would cause them to dip into their nest egg slowly over time. To date, five years into the experiment, this has yet to occur.

Pete and Simi have rejected the standard "if you have it, spend it" way of life in favor of mega-saving. They take time to hunt for bargains (often at consignment shops), grow some of their own food, and do a lot of hands-on work (including the renovations on their small home). They have no land line telephone, no cable television, and only one car, which doesn't see much action. Much of their entertainment comes from a robust computer network crafted by Pete and musical instruments dabbled in by various family members. They aren't alone, as many simple-living books and speakers can tell you, but they are still very different from the cultural norm.

After they had been living this way for some time and getting questions from their friends about how they survive, Pete decided to gather those friends for an informal workshop on their money philosophy. Sitting around the living room at one friend's home, he outlined for them how someone might think differently about purchase decisions. He then worked his audience through the effects of compound interest as applied to "seemingly mundane spending." He took the cost of any weekly spending habit, such as dinner out, and multiplied this over ten years. Combining a mix of various frugality tips, he demonstrated how a typical couple making $140,000 annually could end up with zero savings after ten years with a fairly normal spending pattern, or with $700,000 in savings over the same period—enough to retire if your expenses are low—just by cutting down on expensive luxuries without having any less actual fun.

Pete and Simi, by the way, have a world of fun—together, apart, and as a family with their son, Simon. This includes music and swimming classes for Simon, trips all over the country (often tenting or staying with friends), and outdoor adventures galore. They live quite comfortably, in fact. But they were amazed at the reactions of those friends who came to Pete's workshop that evening. Some were motivated to get started on their own mini-version of saving for retirement; others sat there in disbelief; still others were hostile because the messages were too clearly taken personally. One person asked that Pete never bring up the topic again.

You may have reactions to even our short telling of Pete and Simi's philosophy. Or many questions about how they *really* do it. We could probably write a separate book on their case study (maybe they will consider this themselves someday), but we'll just touch on one question we asked them ourselves: What are they going to do about Simon's college education? Pete had an answer. Their current income responsibly pays for their expenses, and they both have plenty of room to ramp up their earnings if more money is needed. But they do expect Simon to work in advance of college to pay for a lot of it himself, and plan to raise him as a cost-conscious consumer who doesn't place false value on the prestige of a big-name education. Pete considers it vital to teach his son how to provide for himself, most likely through training him in carpentry so that he'll have a fall-back career that can bring in lump sums of money for a few months' work each summer. Before Simon heads off to college, Pete envisions working side by side with his son on a home renovation project or two; the money earned will be Simon's safety net as he starts life on his own. Like the rest of their expenses, college will not be bought with money they don't have.

The Second Rule of ESP spending, then, is an iron-clad imperative to *live below your means*. Track this, watch it, take action if necessary, but don't imprison yourself in worry by owning or doing things you can't afford. Make it a game, like most ESP couples do, and enjoy the good feelings that come from living this way. We're not saying you have to step into complete frugality, but if you want to, you should know you could. By living below your means, you've got all the power to live the life you want.

Spend Consciously

What if you genuinely enjoy eating out every week and don't mind paying for this pleasure? We've already alluded to the idea that prioritizing your spending is a key to living below your means. But this Third Rule of ESP spending is all about the execution. If you now know how much you spend on what, and are paying attention to the bottom line so that you don't spend more than you earn, it seems logical that the next step is to decide exactly how you *want* to spend what you *can* spend. In other words, you'll probably want to set up a budget—a balanced one, of course.

Wait a minute . . . did we just say "budget"?

Yes, alas, we did.

Even more distasteful to many of us than simply tracking expenses is the idea of then binding ourselves to a strict budget, as in, "You can spend only $500 for clothing this year, which means $41.67 per month. This month you've already spent $36 on that new blouse, so you're out of luck if you want to buy those jeans you've been eyeing!" Yuck. So you may be happy to learn that this is *not* what we mean by a budget. The budget of which we speak is another empowerment tool—a plan that gets you where you truly want to be.

Boston ESP dad Imari understands an aversion to budgets, but he is now a full convert to his wife Cynthia's belief in their value and is happy that his wife took the lead in setting one up for their family. Cynthia's success in managing her own money before they met tipped him over to her viewpoint. Now he says, "I often feel like I have *more* money to spend compared to when I was single, thanks to Cynthia's budgeting prowess." Cynthia enthusiastically chimes in: "We're constantly rewarded for budgeting our money by getting to do what we want to do." Together they laugh about "treating our family finances like a business," with financial statements, annual goals, and a yearly budget meeting.

Cynthia and Imari, like many other ESP couples, did the work necessary to set up their finances for success by making their purchases match their priorities through budgeting. Setting up a budget is relatively simple once you've been tracking your spending. Start by assuming that you'll spend exactly the same amount of money in each category (groceries, telephone bill, gas for the car) as you did last year. Then sit down together and do your best guessing at where this assumption doesn't hold water. Just canceled cable TV? You can trim off that cost from your "television" category. Know you need a new suit this year? Add more money to your clothing category. Pretty sure the cost of oil will be going up? Bump up your home heating category. And so on. Think through each category without judgment and with the power of two heads working together. Talk about each adjustment and agree on the new number you'll assign to each category.

Then step back to consider your priorities. Check the Second Rule of ESP spending (*live below your means*) by comparing your newly adjusted expenses to your anticipated income for the coming year. Still balanced? If you notice a shortfall, go back and play with those expenses some more. Come up with some commitments to reduce spending in particular categories, but don't approach these as punitive. Think of them as challenges, like a challenge to bench press a new weight or lose five pounds, and then brainstorm ways in which you might meet the new goals together. If you've got a surplus to spend, similarly think about where you want that money to go—toward college savings, into a new porch for your home, for a family vacation to the shore, or perhaps for a charity of your choice. Then look again at each category from a big-picture view. Would you rather spend your money differently? What if you could shift your work schedule around to spend less on daycare this year, and then spend the windfall on bicycles for the whole family?

If all this sounds onerous, we understand and we're here to alleviate your dread. This budget conversation doesn't have to be an ongoing series of sit-down meetings. In our house, it happens once a year in December and takes about an hour once we print off automated reports of our past year's spending categories. After we've talked, we enter our agreed-on budget numbers for the following year into our financial software, and whenever we're curious, we run a report of how we're doing. We will occasionally rib each other good-naturedly about which one of us is on target for our clothes spending (Marc) and which one of us has blown the clothes budget by April (usually Amy). But all told, we don't "spend" much time on our budget. Of course, if we find ourselves wildly off budget in any category, we'll chat about whether we think that's a good or a bad thing, and what we might do about the discrepancy.

A budget allows you to plan to spend your money according to your values—and skip the regrets of doing otherwise. With ESP, those values are typically to buy extra time to balance out your life—time with your kids, with your spouse, tending your home, on personally rewarding work endeavors, or for your own individual satisfaction. Or sometimes you may want to spend your money to get closer to equality in your partnership. Rather than unconsciously spending increasing amounts of your hard-earned money year after year buying expensive toys for the kids that hardly get played with or fancy gadgets you hardly use, you might spend it this year on an unforgettable family cross-country train trip to see the grandparents. Or not.

While many ESP couples are believers in simple lifestyles, antimaterialism isn't necessarily a goal of ESP. When considering money, the true goal can better be described as consciously prioritized living. Many couples end up becoming proponents of so-called simple living because they realize that much of what we're enticed to buy is not worth the money. But others, like the many ESP couples who value hiring a housecleaning service, find that their costs are still high at this stage in their lives and simply use "consciousness" to prioritize those high costs in the best way for them. We could continue to write pages and pages (a whole book, surely) on ways to prioritize spending, but luckily many others have already done so. We've listed a couple of our favorite voices in "Additional Reading," but we also encourage you to seek out this information from a wide variety of sources.

Breaking the Money Barrier

Mary Ellen and Ariel, the nurse and housepainter ESP couple with four children, both come from relatively underprivileged families. Growing up, neither of them knew the excitement of a trip away during school-break weeks or summer vacation, and their traditional parents had little spare change for luxuries. So now that they are parents themselves, they laugh when others see their lives as "voluntary simplicity." "We both feel so well off now. Sure, money gets tighter with each child who joins our family, but compared to our childhoods, we're rich!" says Mary Ellen. This kind of perspective is not something we're used to applying to money, but it can be a powerful force in breaking the money arguments against ESP.

The happiness literature is pretty much in agreement with the old saying that money doesn't buy, um, happiness. If you're so poor that you cannot afford basic needs, such as food, water, shelter, and clothes, money will indeed improve your life, but beyond this stage, it may, in fact, take you farther from what truly gives you joy. Some ESP couples are pretty well off, while others get by with far less than most people consider reasonable income. All prioritize their decisions about how to work and how to spend with an eye toward creating and keeping the lifestyle they want— not in the usual sense of "lifestyle to which they've become accustomed" but in the sense of equal partnership and everyday balance.

How much is ESP worth to you? When you do the math, you find out how much it might cost you to live in various ways. Sometimes ESP costs less than more standard parenting options—hooray! Sometimes it can cost about the same. Sometimes it can cost more—but now you can estimate how *much* more. What if your ideal life would cost the family $2,000 more annually? Would you pay this? How about $4,000? $10,000? Consider what you'd get for your money—perhaps more time with your kids, more intimacy with your partner, less stress, a meaningful career or a less all-consuming one, a less chaotic home, enough time for yourself. Consider the price, and compare it to other ways you currently spend that money. Can you even afford this cost? What would you give up to make this possible? There is no right answer to any of these questions. But like everything, ESP often has a price tag, and your decision to buy or pass it up should be made with open eyes.

ESP couples break the money barrier by using a combination of the rules in this chapter. They play with their work schedules to optimize their income within boundaries that they consciously build—around how much time they want to devote to their children, themselves, and their home, and how much money they truly need to purchase what aligns with their core values. They know where they spend their money, and they don't finance their lifestyle by going into debt or by buying without thinking. Many non-ESP families use these methods of money management, too—they are common sense. But put them together with a priority for equal partnership and balanced lives, and you've got affordable ESP!

Breaking through the barrier that money puts up against ESP can be extremely difficult, especially if you've got a lot invested in your current way of life. But it isn't that you can't afford ESP. It isn't that your life just costs too much or that your job just pays too little. The problem doesn't, after all is analyzed, reside in money. You have plenty—more than many. Your kids will be fine if you downgrade their expenses (even a bit of their college savings!) and ramp up your time with them as two equal and happy parents instead. Making your money work for you means using what you have to create the life you love. So use it wisely.

Society

COURAGE TO CHANGE/WISDOM TO NOTICE

Carl loved to take his children to the grocery store when they were young. But he had one hard-and-fast rule: If you *ask* Daddy for anything, you will not get it; but if you *don't* ask, he will buy you a little something special just before getting in the checkout line. With this rule, he and his two daughters, Rebecca and Alison, enjoyed years' worth of excursions down the aisles. Yet one trip in particular stands out in Carl's mind. It happened when Rebecca was about six years old—a new reader who suddenly noticed words everywhere around her. As they entered their usual supermarket, she spied something just her size—a new batch of mini–shopping carts sitting right alongside the grown-ups' carts, all under a big sign that said MOMMY'S LITTLE HELPER.

Rebecca took a cart and marched ahead of her father and sister to the customer service desk. "Dads shop, too," she patiently explained. The next time Carl and his daughters visited that store, the sign had been changed to PARENT'S LITTLE HELPER.

All around us, society sets up expectations, and unsuspecting (and, we like to think, innocent) people, businesses, and organizations follow along. Social expectations grow out of how our neighborhoods, larger communities, gender, ethnicity, race, religion, age, profession, socioeconomic class, health status, sexual preference, and family background are viewed by ourselves and others. Some expectations universally make sense—such as the assumption that people with diabetes want to be careful about what they eat—but many are way off the mark. Families, in particular, come in so many shapes and sizes that treating them alike can result in anything from mild amusement to frustration to harm for those who are different from the "norm."

The most exasperating part about social expectations is that they are so often mistaken for solid truth. Gendered roles, for example, are the subject of innumerable books, research papers, and women's studies lectures, yet every day we all unthinkingly commit "crimes" of judgment based on gender as we walk, talk, and breathe. Who decided men should never wear skirts, and why aren't they free to choose differently? Why, in an age of acceptable voluntary male baldness, do our minds have room for bald women only if they have cancer? How many of us, upon noticing a lone male parent's name on our children's classroom contact list, would assume that some terrible ill had befallen the poor child's mother? The problem is not that men's bodies are incapable of wearing skirts or that a razor will not cut women's hair or that men can't act as the go-to parent at their children's schools. It is that we operate under a set of social rules seemingly as powerful to us as the physical world.

In small ways and very big ones, embracing a life of equally shared parenting means having to traverse many social expectations and assumptions. ESP is still mostly invisible to the outside world. We're typically not out there drawing attention to our differences or furiously sewing skirts in men's sizes, but no matter our age, ethnicity, or social peer group, chances are we stand out as a wee bit different once other parents, coworkers, and even our own siblings and parents get to know how our families function on a daily basis.

To a couple who vaguely wishes to move in the direction of equal sharing, getting past social norms can seem difficult. And sometimes it truly is. But the happy news is that to established ESP parents, social barriers are more of a simple annoyance at times, a source of humor at other times, a chance for advocacy perhaps, a puzzle to solve, or at worst, a setback to tackle. Grocery carts labeled to appeal to the majority of parents who shop at a particular store are hardly an affront to the reality of ESP; we know that ESP couples determined to carve out lives of equality and balance will not be stopped by a label that doesn't fit their beliefs. But if that little label stands for a whole society that says women do all the shopping, it becomes a quietly powerful deterrent to setting up a family structure encouraging equitable access to the grocery store.

Social barriers to ESP, then, just like the money barriers we discussed in the previous chapter, are mirages. They look real, and if taken at face value, they can undermine your personal quest for an equal partnership. Yet when you are personally ready to take them on, you can make them vanish. Social barriers, specifically, are prone to creep up on couples, and slowly erode their equal sharing plans when they aren't watching. So we've saved this discussion for last, as a final step that is best addressed only *after* you understand how ESP will work in the context of your own family.

In this chapter, we'll examine some of the ways that society is set up to discourage this life we treasure. You already know that a pledge to ESP includes the willingness and courage to circumvent cultural traps, so here we'll focus on giving you specific action steps to do that. We'll begin by taking notice of how our world caters to traditional motherhood, and then move to fatherhood; along the way, we'll show you how you can live harmoniously in such a world while holding tight to equality and balance.

The Mommy Club

Most of us like the grounding feeling that comes from belonging. Legitimate membership in an exclusive group can make us feel like we've "arrived" and can give us the chance to bond over our challenges—making them feel suddenly doable or simply normal. We are no longer alone when we can connect with our peers. Such is the case when a woman gives birth (or adopts) and steps into the world's largest exclusive alliance—what we call the Mommy Club.

As with any like-minded group, the Mommy Club has its noble purposes—such as women helping other women to navigate all the difficulties of motherhood—but it is also responsible for many of the cultural barriers to ESP. Mothers connect with other mothers in many ways, both formally in new moms' groups and Mommy & Me classes, and informally as they chat at school pickup time, during playdates, or at the library. Mom to mom, these women often relate to each other unconsciously (or sometimes quite obviously) as *the* parent in their children's lives—the one who knows how to do it right, makes all the decisions, understands her children's cries, tears her hair out on the tough days, and has to put up with the inferior parenting of her mate.

Rather than wrap ourselves in the comfy cocoon of the Mommy Club, ESP moms must instead learn to align ourselves equally with parents of either gender. Yes, we remain mothers and our husbands remain fathers (in opposition to when sociologists sometimes use the term "mothering" to refer to any parent nurturing his or her children), and we may enjoy getting together with other moms just as much as any traditional mother might do. But we have the distinct task of stepping around the cliquey nature of motherhood. Except for when referring to true biological differences, such as pregnancy, childbirth, and breastfeeding, we must learn to substitute the word "parent" for the word "mother" as we move through our days.

Where does "mother" show up and wreak ESP havoc? Everywhere! Mom-centered biases in the ordinary world take the form of physical, mental, and attitudinal barriers to male childraising and housework. And for an ESP couple, surmounting these barriers means three pieces of extra work: transferring knowledge to *keep fathers informed, rising above judgment* from others, and *resisting stereotypes*. Let's take a closer look at each of these tactics.

Keeping Fathers Informed

From caregivers and parents to coaches and the PTA, outsiders connect mostly with moms. The pediatrician might address only

Mom at visits attended by both of you or, worse yet, bend down to your toddler's eye level and say something like, "Now, you tell Mommy that you need to take this medicine two times every day, okay?" when Dad is the sole parent at the visit. It can be Mom who gets the calls to arrange playdates, even if Dad answers the phone. Or Mom who is asked to coordinate the school bake sale, make the banner for the soccer team, or bring in the snacks—again—while Dad has to call twice to successfully volunteer. And then there's your kid's best friend's mother who reaches out only to Mom with the scoop on the application deadline for that hard-to-get new summer camp.

At our children's schools, moms are placed on email lists and signed up for autocalls to their cell phones when their children arrive late or there is a start delay for bad weather. Even when both parents provide their contact information, or when Dad works from home and Mom's job is an hour's drive away, mothers find themselves in the information chain far more often than fathers. And consequently, moms can have an easier job than dads staying "in the know" about their children's schedules and learning progress—and all the little school rules, regulations, and deadlines that make it possible to participate in a helpful and meaningful way.

Businesses that sell child-related goods and services market their wares to mothers, parenting magazines might as well be re-named "moms-only" magazines for their paucity of father-directed content, and household cleaning products and services are sold with similar philosophies. Without any effort, and sometimes without their consent, ESP moms are barraged with information; ESP dads, on the other hand, must often seek it out. These business moves make sense; after all, companies want to cater to their primary buyers—mothers (or women in general).

And when traditional moms—and the caregivers used to speaking with these traditional moms—mistake us for more of the same, we can't really blame them. How were they to know differently? We can't, therefore, seriously ask marketers or even schools, doctors, or other parents to stop appealing to the majority en masse.

As ESP mothers and fathers, however, we can take simple steps to guard against letting this moms-only information highway leave our own relationships lopsided. And guard we must, for the more mothers are given the details of the school's lunch menu or the pediatric vaccine schedule, the more mothers become saddled with the first-pass decision making about these facts. "Should I pack a lunch for tomorrow, or is it pizza day?" "When do I need to schedule that next doctor's appointment?" "When did the teacher say we had to turn in the field trip forms?" If Mom automatically gets all the details, or comes by them with very little effort, a couple can easily lapse into naming her the family's main source of household information. Slowly, without any premeditation, even dedicated ESP fathers can begin to defer at home and with the kids, and their information-loaded partners can begin to take charge.

Sometimes ESP couples fight the system by correcting email lists to include both parents or by politely passing the phone back to Dad to negotiate the details of a playdate being scheduled on his watch. Sometimes they build in their own homegrown safeguards, such as making sure that all papers coming home from school are placed in a designated spot and sifted through by both partners. Other times Mom simply relays information to Dad— but is careful to minimize ownership of the information if it wasn't hers to own; for example, she simply forwards an email he might need to read without also coaching him on exactly what details are important and why. Finally, an ESP mom might give in and retain responsibility for some of the tasks that life hands her anyway, as long as the overall workload of childraising and housework remains equally shared.

Dads can take proactive aim at the information problem as well. By recognizing that they may be cheated out of key information, ESP fathers venturing into stereotypical mom territory must often take responsibility for asking and bear the burden of the extra work that comes with this responsibility. Simply inquiring "Is there anything I need to know?" can often get you up to speed when you sign up to bring in the class Valentine cupcakes. Then, and only then, you might be told that two children are allergic to wheat, one to peanuts, and one doesn't do dairy—and how previous cupcake-baking parents have handled this (chances are these facts were broadcast earlier on the moms-only cupcake information channel). So, read what useful information does come your way, and ask for the rest from the school, the pediatrician, your partner, and your kids!

Rising Above Judgment

We are undoubtedly all aware that much of the housework and childraising tasks reflect on mothers in our society. If the home is messy or dirty or unsafe, chances are Mom will feel the glare of judgment—whether real or imagined—from those who notice. If the kids are wearing clothes that don't fit or refuse to wear their coats in the dead of winter, we can all imagine that Mom might be the first one blamed (and even if the issue is noticed on Dad's watch, Mom could be judged for inappropriately delegating the task to her husband). Of course, we also know that it is our job as ESP parents to ignore these judgments—to indeed rise above them, brush them off, and carry on with our equal sharing.

But how might we lessen the societal blow we must endure? And even more importantly, how can we shield our relationships from sliding into inequality simply as an avoidance mechanism? No parent is a saint. So when faced with enough time to mow the lawn or bathe the children, even the most committed ESP mother might choose to run the bath water; the unkempt grass will reflect more on her husband than on her, but stinky, grimy children . . . Likewise, an ESP father might be tempted to haul out the lawn mower and let the kids' baths wait until tomorrow. Over time, this understandable behavior can grate against an otherwise equal relationship, and a couple could easily revert to traditional roles even when they wish otherwise. While it is fine to designate lawn mowing to men and bathing to women, the problem arises when we let social pressures—not our own preferences—make the assignment.

To battle against the effects of societal judgment, ESP couples find it helpful to stay aware when this might happen. If you know you're taking on a traditionally opposite-gendered task, for instance, you might take extra care with your responsibilities. If an ESP father volunteers to bake the turkey for Thanksgiving dinner with his in-laws, for example, he should be well aware that the stakes may be a bit higher for follow-through than if he takes responsibility for next Thursday's grilled cheese lunches with the kids. ESP couples can also avoid much of the social stare-down by simply removing themselves from the scene, such as one mom who is "conveniently absent on a day when my mother-in-law visits so that I'm not there to take any blame for the state of the house or the outfits my children are wearing."

Of course, no ESP family should live for how others might

be judging them. ESP mom Helena advises that we simply "practice going against societal expectations and learn to care less about things that don't really matter." ESP mom Mary Ellen, whose husband creates handmade Halloween costumes and coordinates the birthday parties for their four children each year, advises that mothers actually take delight in our husbands' handling of jobs that society says are hallmarks of a good mother. Even a botched Thanksgiving turkey or a messy home can become the best of stories and can serve to share with others how your own family ticks. In fact, ESP couples typically plow through their discomfort until it becomes second nature to ignore cultural judgment.

There is one important caveat, however. Rising above external judgment should not be confused with settling for an unacceptable result for any task in your home or with your children. If how the turkey is cooked, or what the children are wearing to your cousin's wedding, matters deeply to *you*, you have a right (and a responsibility) to speak up when your spouse crosses the line. The key here is understanding whether your anxiety comes from societal discomfort or from truly taking pleasure in doing something

SHARING WHEN THE WORLD IS LOOKING AT YOU: A MESSAGE FROM AMY

Shunning societal expectation can be an especially awkward and public lesson in letting go. Like many women, for example, I tend to take the lead in picking out the menu, shopping for the food, cooking, and generally planning an evening when guests are expected. And

Marc, like most men, assists under my direction. But one day we talked about how this pattern felt too traditional to us and decided that the next time we formally invited a friend for dinner, we would switch things up. The result: leftovers. Not leftovers as in an almost full pan of home-baked lasagna. Leftovers as in "empty the fridge and serve up what we have." Some of us got to finish off the baked squash from last night, while others dug into the leftover pasta. Dessert was the end of a package of store-bought cookies.

Now mind you—this is *not* my way. I'll be the first to admit to cringing at Marc's plans when I got wind of them. But I could tell that Marc didn't serve leftovers out of spite or to teach me a "lesson." He made this decision because this is the way he would have put together a meal for a guest if he were a bachelor.

I learned through this experiment that there is room for Marc's way too, and that it is *my* job—my ESP burden, if you will—to get past my societal discomfort. In Marc's world, serving a good friend (as this guest was) leftovers is like saying "you are part of our family." To him, this is an honor. In the end, after I was able to shake off the feeling that I might be judged or that my way was the *only* way to treat a guest well, I found that I could relax into enjoying our friend's company and let Marc take the kudos (or blame) for the details.

It takes two people to make equal sharing work, and the social barriers are often subtle. In this example, we could have gone on forever in our usual unequal dinner-for-guest work division without too many problems, but putting ourselves up to challenges like this reaffirms that ESP means more to us than the judgment (real or perceived) of others. Marc also got to share the anxiety, however slight, of preparing for a guest, and I learned a few things about being in the helper role.

to a different standard. Your delivery is crucial, too; approaching the topic by sharing your desired outcome and negotiating an acceptable standard with your partner goes a lot further than accusing your partner of being a social neophyte.

Resisting Stereotypes

The world is full of bumbling dad images from sitcoms and movies—men who can't be trusted to stay home with a baby and don't know the first thing about how to maneuver a vacuum. And scenes of air-headed women unable to hammer a nail or understand a tax return. These are obvious stereotypes—probably still existing in the flesh somewhere but certainly not in most homes. Yet less obvious stereotyping happens all the time in conversation and in how society expects men and women to act. These stereotypes contain a grain of truth because they remain accurate for many traditional couples; they are just no longer true for ESP families, and understanding how they may be harmful to our equality is an important step in letting them go.

Take, for example, those syrupy chain letters that make their way around most women's email in-boxes. If you're a mom, you will probably know instantly what we're talking about—those odes to motherhood sent by well-meaning female friends that showcase how hard moms work and how clueless our husbands are to our sacrifices. All mothers, the words intone, are pillars of strength and wisdom as they tend to their children's every need while their spouses remain blissfully unaware that the children have needs at all. Moms rule, dads drool! A huge high-five to all mothers—those fantastic creatures, those martyred souls—who have to do it all *and* put up with their inept husbands. At the end of these emails, we're encouraged to forward the message to all our friends so we can brighten their day just as ours has clearly been enriched.

We doubt anyone escapes the opportunity to actively or passively partake in a little spouse bashing—deserved or not.

KEEPING QUIET

I t feels good to be able to talk to someone about all of this! We can't talk like this in our everyday world. We'd sound too preachy, too righteous. We'd give off a weird vibe." So say Melissa and Richard when we ask them to tell us about their lives, and we've heard similar words from a remarkable number of other ESP couples we've come to know. "My maternity leave was a dream time; my girlfriends complained bitterly about theirs." "Whenever I get together with my friends, the first words out of their mouths are always about how hard it was to leave the house and leave the kids with their husbands." "When we tell others about how much quality time we have, it feels a bit like when some people talk about how much money they have—it's a blessing that we want to shout from the rooftops, but it seems like bragging if we do." We hear words like these over and over.

There is so much about ESP that goes against our culture—men who nurture children as much as they work, men who tend their home with gusto even though their gender could exempt them from this task, women who don't hold fast to directing the home and raising the kids. Add in the anticonsumerist subculture of many ESP families and their redefinition of success toward balance rather than worldly achievement, and you've got a volatile mix sure to appear "holier than thou" to many.

While ESP parents hope every couple can structure their lives to the satisfaction of both partners, and they don't pretend to have the fits-all answer to happiness, most would rather not risk others thinking they feel differently. You may feel the same way as you move through your days, but we have hope that this isolation is waning. Even in the three years since we've begun to speak out about ESP, we've noticed that it has become an increasingly common topic of discussion. As it feels safe to do, we recommend you *don't* keep quiet. By letting others know about the good *and* tough parts of your shared life, you may find support and connection—and an honest ability to help others realize their dreams—in the most surprising places.

But without minimizing the difficulties of parents who don't have capable and willing partners to share the load—God knows life can be difficult for *any* of us at times—ESP parents have to be careful not to follow suit to fit in. Moms could forward those martyred mommy emails as instructed. They could laugh along with the sitcoms or the McDonald's advertisement showing its products as the natural answer to dinner on the rare night Dad is supposed to cook. Dads might be tempted to chuckle along with the colleague who constantly refers to his wife as a ball and chain and his kids only as rugrats. What's the harm, right? To ESP parents, this humor misses the mark—it is simply neither interesting nor funny. And while we may not jump up in indignation and leave the room or launch into a sermon when the dumb husband or stupid wife jokes start, we understand deep down that participating means nibbling at the roots of what we have so carefully built.

The Daddy Pass

When Dorea's wife, Angela, gave birth to their daughter, Dorea was determined to be a full coparent—a mother just as legitimate as the world considered her partner. It was Dorea who went to the local new moms' group, for example, and sat among all the biological new mothers who spoke about how tired they felt. Dorea listened with interest and empathy, but heard something she found rather disconcerting. More than one of these moms had excused her husband from much of the grunt work of parenting—any part in the middle-of-the-night duties, for example—on the grounds that he was a graduate student. Graduate students, these mothers seemed to believe, were in special need of their sleep and their own time.

Dorea took in their comments and then challenged them. "I'm a graduate student," she revealed. She then explained that rather than impeding shared workloads at home, her graduate studies were part of what made her available to coparent. "It's amazing that these families allowed the myth of male graduate student sanctity to be so real for them," she mused later to us. "Would they have made this automatic assumption if the mothers themselves had been the students?"

Even if we cut the fathers some slack—assume they weren't the ones vehemently objecting to changing a diaper—we can see how both parents could have internalized the cultural expectation of Mom as the parent who should take the brunt of sleep deprivation and baby chores. Even new fathers who plan to dig into parenthood could easily fall for the idea that they are more needed elsewhere—be they graduate students, medical residents, programmers, or workers in just about any job that requires an awake human. When this idea comes from within the marriage, we'll refer you back to Chapter 4 to crush it down. But when the notion sneaks up from the outside—from how our culture tells fathers that they have a free pass out of "real" parenthood—then we'd better learn to deflect it here.

We've given a name to our society's acceptance of a father opting out of equal involvement in childraising and homemaking: the Daddy Pass. Even when an ESP father has no intention—or desire—to use it, our culture will present him with it time and again. It will be dangled in front of him, and when the baby has been crying for two hours and the dishes are piled up in the sink, it can actually look quite attractive. Both he *and* his wife can get tricked, like the families Dorea spoke of, into thinking he's off the hook and she's more responsible. Just as with mom-centered biases, therefore, the Daddy Pass represents physical, mental, or attitudinal barriers to equal sharing and all the riches that come from a balanced life. Let's look at three ways that both men and women can avoid cashing in the Daddy Pass: *innovating childcare* so that fathers get what they need, *redirecting praise* from others, and setting *autopilot equality* patterns that nourish ESP instead.

Innovating Childcare

Ask any involved father about the adventures of diaper changing outside the home, and you'll probably get a funny story. While it can be hard enough to find a clean, safe place to lay a baby when you're his mother, it is often downright comical to consider what fathers have to juggle to change a diaper in most men's rooms (some terrific exceptions notwithstanding). The world is set up to accommodate mothers—sometimes—but solo parenting by Dad can be ever the exercise in innovation.

ESP dads have been rejected from new moms' groups and purposefully not invited to playgroups. They have been ignored by other parents on the playground. Parenting books (and magazines, as we've mentioned) are written for women, often with puny sections for fathers devoted mostly to how they can assist their wives. Even in social situations where dads are freely welcome, they are still typically in the minority (barring the occasional father-daughter dance or father-son camping trip). An ESP dad, therefore, comes to expect that whenever he takes the kids to children's music hour at the bookstore, he could well be the only adult male there. Chances are he'll spot other men hanging out with their children at the park from time to time, but the statistical likelihood he'll bond with them is far lower than the average mom's probability of meeting a new friend. And forging lasting friendships with other moms will take most guys only so far.

So most ESP dads (like stay-at-home dads) will challenge themselves to get past these issues because they don't like the alternatives: venturing out in isolation, or slowly shrinking their time with the kids to a more private sphere, while their wives enjoy fully public, socially supported mothering. By making it a bit harder for men to care for their children in public and to surround themselves with supportive others, our culture hands fathers their pass out. Instead of accepting, ESP fathers get innovative.

Jonathan is one ESP dad who found ways around the mom-focused parenting world. He fondly remembers how he was welcomed to his eldest daughter Emily's school by volunteering to teach her fourth grade class about an early computer software program. Because the veteran teacher did not feel comfortable with computers back then, Jonathan was able to turn his availability and willingness into a weekly gig at the school. And years before, finding himself the only man at the library's toddler drop-in time, Jonathan joined a few other men—mostly academic types at the time—to talk about "doing fathering differently." The group ended up meeting monthly for eighteen years!

Carl, little Rebecca's father, used a similar tactic to gain acceptance in his local babysitting co-op. First he simply joined the group and volunteered to help out with odd jobs: typing lists, making the cards used for currency, hosting a coffee hour to introduce a new member family. Then, when the group's coordinator moved away, he raised his hand to become the new leader. "It was easy for me to take over, as everybody knew me and knew

I would do what I said I would," says Carl. "The fact that I was male was less relevant by that time."

Bruce, another ESP dad, gets in on the playdate circuit by first offering to be the host—and inviting multiple little friends over at once for the biggest impact. "Then they know me and owe me," says Bruce. Sure enough, pretty soon he's off and runnin' with the moms.

Jon, Carl, and Bruce, and many other ESP dads, advocate getting involved in typically moms-only parenting realms by

MEN AT WORK

While this chapter's main focus is on social barriers to equal child-raising and homemaking, we are all aware that pressures against ESP in the *workplace* can be just as strong. Stereotypically, these are worst for men, who fear ridicule or even job security if they take their company's allowed paternity leave or put in a request for reduced or flexible hours so that they can be home with their kids. As we discussed earlier, the benefits to these moves far outweigh the risks for most of us. But sometimes work expectations for men can seep into our relationships in forms such as an ESP father hiding his intentions when he leaves early to scoop up a sick child from preschool. Or even in deferring this responsibility more often to his wife solely because this behavior will be more culturally tolerated coming from her.

There's no comfortable answer to these unfortunate pressures. It isn't fair for us to suggest you should always own up to your ESP beliefs in the face of true job risk. But the more often you can do so when the stakes aren't quite so high, the easier it will be to do the next time. Don't apologize for your values or back away from living them to please a work culture that's behind the times. Don't flaunt your balanced life either, of course, but look for opportunities to make it seem unflinchingly normal. And be a role model when you can—it feels great to help another guy stand up for what he really wants from life.

gradually proving themselves trustworthy, proactive, and willing, rather than by a "frontal assault." But sometimes a man has to do what he has to do. When the only diapering facilities at the amusement park are labeled "Mama's House," the bench right outside will have to do the trick.

Redirecting Praise

Although the sight of a man pushing a baby stroller is no longer considered a miracle, there is still a well-known chasm between how men and women are viewed by strangers when they parent in public. For women, caring for children is considered a natural duty and privilege. For men, it is often considered an isn't-that-sweet, just-babysitting-to-give-his-wife-a-break activity. Traditionally, this dichotomy gives fathers tremendous leeway to handle solo-parenting time without taking on much responsibility or worrying about looking like a poor parent. The bar to succeed is very low! Furthermore, the praise that any decent display of fathering can elicit from others can feel great.

The same can be said about housework, at least when we consider the household chores most commonly done by women. Society still says that a man who routinely washes, cooks, cleans, and does laundry is a tremendous catch, and a woman who finds herself "lucky" enough to snag such a man had better be forever thankful. It's nowhere near as common to hear a man express his fortune in finding a woman who handles her share of these tasks.

But beware! When compliments are lavished on an ESP dad for the same tasks an ESP mom is simply expected to handle, inequality can creep into the relationship. This injustice itself is not likely to be the undoing of equal sharing for any committed couple, but it is important to notice the issue and call it for what it is: incorrect. Not noticing this social vestige of traditional gender roles—or worse yet, welcoming and believing the praise—is a Daddy Pass move that says "for men, parenting and housework are only optional." It is a short step from there to believing it, even just a little.

ESP dads, while they may not attempt to stir things up among their friends, do find cute and sometimes humorous ways to redirect praise given to them for just doing their share. Sam, who frequents library sing-alongs with his four-year-old, developed a standard response when mothers would coo their approval at his presence and actually thank him for attending. "And thank *you* for coming today, too," he would reply, adding, "I really enjoy it—I feel lucky to be here." Or take the case of envy mixed with confusion that ESP mom Megan received once when she showed up to her book club meeting with homemade cornbread—matter-of-factly baked from scratch by her husband, Marco, earlier that day. "When it started to win compliments at the meeting, I had to fess up that I didn't make it. Everyone in the room was amazed that Marco was willing to make something for me to bring, especially when he was the one at home putting the kids to bed while I drank wine with my friends." While Marco wasn't there to accept or reject their looks of awe, Megan took the compliments gracefully and filled him in when she got home. They both chuckled at the level of amazement created by such a simple thing and at how low the standards can be for men's home involvement. Megan knew that if a guy showed up at a potluck with his wife's macaroni salad, no one would blink an eye. She hoped her book club friends could now begin to see the cornbread this way, too.

ESP parents redirect praise by simply acting as if what they are doing is perfectly normal—which it is. They don't internalize

EMPLOYEE OF THE MONTH

Praise isn't just misaligned with an ESP life at the sing-a-long or in the kitchen. At work, highest honors are often given to employees who are role models for unbalanced lives, and most of the time no one seems to notice this crazy thinking. "This certificate goes to Joe Smith, who never leaves before seven p.m., and even came in every weekend last quarter to get the ABC project completed ahead of schedule," a manager might gush at a typical company's annual awards ceremony. Forget about Sally or Dave, who felt no need to jeopardize their family lives or their personal time, and simply worked more efficiently instead.

We hope, over time, that more companies will come to value top-notch work more than simply overwork, but in the meantime we can all attempt to resist the siren song of these kinds of rewards. If you're a manager, don't follow suit as you select worthy recipients. If you're not, just keep your wits and continue to be a truly fantastic employee. And really, who needs a silly certificate anyway?

it as unequal gratitude—"I'm so lucky to have a husband who does so much"—or expect appreciation for doing what brings them a joyful life—"You should be thankful I'm not like ninety-nine percent of the other guys!" Appreciation plays a huge role in their relationship, but not as a way to stroke anyone's ego or as currency that assures they stick to doing their share.

Autopilot Equality

With all the social expectations nudging fathers to accept an easy out from down-and-dirty childraising, housework, and other jobs traditionally handed to women, some ESP couples find it hard to stay vigilant against the tide. They manage well enough most days, but every so often they will look up and notice that they've drifted toward standard gender roles without their conscious consent. As we've said before, mindful decisions to follow customary male-female chore division are no problem; in our house, for example, Marc tends to do the lawn mowing 90 percent of the time and Amy tends to plan almost all of our dinner parties (switch-ups aside). But to a couple who clearly wishes to share a typically gendered task more evenly, or to assign it to the atypically gendered spouse, abdication of this plan owing to social pressure is a big letdown.

To combat a slow slide into tradition, and yet avoid constant watchfulness and suspicion, many ESP couples build concrete patterns and customs for their families that reflect their desires for equality and balance. Helena and Domenico, for example, noticed that when almost any couple drives to a destination together, it is the man who hops behind the wheel of the car. So they created their own overriding custom: when driving *to* a destination, Helena sits in the driver's seat, and when driving *home*, Domenico takes over. Once in place, Helena and Domenico's simple personal tradition of shared driving serves to short-circuit the automatic pull of male automotive privilege without much effort from either of them.

Other ESP couples find fun and interesting ways to create their own traditions, too. We've met couples who take turns pushing the stroller when they walk together, switch spots at the dining room table so that both parents can take turns feeding the baby, assign grocery shopping to the spouse who didn't make the shopping list, or alternate who gets up with the kids and who can sleep in. Our own daily life is full of homemade customs that allow us to automate equal sharing, such as our set pattern of putting our children to bed (most often, we each take one child, switching every other day; Sundays are kids' choice), or our

THE PROBLEM OF LAST NAMES

OOne topic that ESP couples find difficult to tease apart from tradition is how to choose a last name for their children. Custom says it should be the father's surname; feminism says "not so fast." Hyphens sometimes work, but they become hard to carry into further generations. Choosing the mother's name is an option, but then we've reversed the problem just to avoid societal expectations. Giving different names to each child? Could be confusing. Making up a whole new name for the family? Then you lose some of the nice parts of tradition—if you value a concrete link to your genealogy. There is, we're convinced, no perfect solution.

Many ESP couples do succeed in bucking tradition in favor of what works best for them. There's the couple who combined his last name (Hopper) with hers (Smith) to create the unique surname of Hoppersmith for their children. There is the couple who each took the other's last name (Zobal or Dent) as their own middle name upon marriage, and did the same for each of their two children (meaning there are now two Zobal Dent family members and two who are Dent Zobals). And then there are Carl and Debby. Carl's last name is hard to spell, is hard to pronounce, and includes the prefix "von." Debby's, in contrast, is as simple as you can get. So they immediately agreed that they would choose Debby's name for their children. This turned out to be quite a challenge, however, since they lived in the last Canadian province that then required all married couples' children to bear the husband's last name. Carl and Debby fought back, joining together with separated moms who also disagreed with the law, and took the issue to their provincial human rights commission. Their case wended through the legal system for four years, but they got the law changed. Carl and Debby's two daughters bear the last name Lake.

now-defunct 2:00 a.m. cutoff for which parent responded to a baby's wails. The idea behind setting your own ESP customs or traditions is to make it as easy as possible to stay the course of equal sharing without having to think about it. Why make life difficult?

Scaling the Society Barrier
Toward Activism

Society gives us all a set of rules to follow and a set of roles to assume. I'll be the breadwinner and wear the pants; you raise the children and wear the skirts. I'll come to the kids' ballet recital and coach their basketball practices; you show up at their basketball games and bring them to their weekly ballet classes. These traditional rules and roles require very little resistance, since our culture fully supports them, and they can be assumed almost unconsciously.

ESP asks couples to think way bigger, however. For the twin prizes of equality and balance, and all the riches that these bring to your parenting, your career, your home, your relationship, and yourself, the effort required by you to think past social norms is well invested—so much so that you may find yourself, like many ESP couples, becoming an activist of sorts. Some couples start out that way, of course, choosing equally shared parenting as a natural extension of their profeminist values and actions or of their general discomfort with being like everyone else. But others are called to social activism later, by their deep belief in the beauty of ESP.

Activism can take many forms. For us, it means launching our website and writing this book—devoting our free time to bringing ESP out into the light of day. For others, it can mean gently suggesting to friends that specific cultural norms are not set in stone—quietly bringing up an alternative to a working-mom colleague, for example, who complains about always being the one to leave work to go home when her kids have school early-release days. For many, it means speaking up to businesses that discourage male parenting, such as registering a formal request for a changing table in the men's bathroom at their favorite local restaurant. Or complaining to the staff at a meal preparation business that decorates its stores with "cute" pejorative quotes about men in the kitchen.

Activism can also be taken up simply by living publicly as an ESP mother or father, such as David, the physician who negotiated for part-time hours when he joined his nephrology practice and has now passively influenced more than half of his colleagues to do the same. Or it can mean living proudly as an ESP-minded individual in your own extended family. Many ESP couples have stories to tell about how their own parents reacted to their decisions to share equally in childraising and to cut back from power careers to do so. "What will you *do* with all that time?" asked one career-oriented father upon hearing of his son's plans to be home two days every week with his new baby.

Finally, there are the child activists. Like little Rebecca in the grocery store, ESP children have been known to take up the cause from time to time. We have had the privilege of hearing about, listening to, and even meeting some of the older children of ESP families, and are universally impressed with their understanding of barriers to equality in their own social circles. They may choose to stick with "safe" gender roles during adolescence (a very hard time to experiment!), but they know their own families stand for something else. When they get a bit older, they seem more aware of these issues than your average young adult, and we've known

ESP DATING

Our anti-equality culture is at work on us well before we entertain thoughts of settling down and having children. Have you ever considered that it is kind of crazy to be out there in the dating world, searching for an equal partner, and yet abiding by old social rules that encourage inequality? Men pursue, women succumb. Men pay, women say "thank you" (in so many ways). Men puff up their macho, financially successful, provider selves to attract women, and women polish their images as doting girlfriends and aim to please by their physical appearance. We're encouraged to marry up or marry down depending on our gender; trophy husbands are rich (and could be reticent to share the breadwinning equally), and trophy wives are young, sexy, and able to keep a beautiful home. Yikes. These are generalizations, surely, but it's no wonder the dating game can send mixed messages if we then expect our significant others to morph into equal partners after marriage and children!

It can be hard to buck dating and mating traditions, and we open ourselves up to all sorts of subliminal judgment when we try to act differently—"too" wimpy or "too" aggressive for our gender. But the one requirement for ESP to germinate is that you have two willing partners. If you value a life of equality and balance, then your core happiness depends on at least bending those traditions to avoid future confusion, and choosing your life partner wisely.

Most ESP couples report that they were relatively mainstream in their courtship days, but advise anyone in the dating scene who wants an ESP future to shoot for:

Equal financial responsibility. Fine, he can pay for the first date—or not—but there's no need to continue this practice after that.

Equal career values. Concentrate on dating your peers—those with similarly important and demanding career choices—so that you're in less danger of placing one partner's career ahead of the other's later on.

A shared vision of a good life. Forget about waxing poetic that you and your date share an interest in gourmet cooking or Shakespeare! What matters for ESP is that you both want this kind of life more than anything; this shared vision is what will prevent one of you from having to drag the other along when the going gets tough.

more than one to gravitate toward a career in social activism or to carefully select a future mate who will embrace equality alongside them.

Any public stance, on just about any issue, can bring out criticism and even hatred. If done in a way that denigrates the choices of others, it is worthy of some backlash. But if done in the spirit of expanding societal options to fit better with the diversity of families in the community, and without unreasonable demands, it is wholly positive and a service to all. An ESP activist, or anyone who gets out there to promote equal rights and expose gender bias, is a public servant.

Strength in Numbers

Thankfully, we've come a long way from the days when it was a social taboo for women to work or for men to spend any decent time nurturing their children or cleaning the home. But the vestiges of those social expectations still linger—in the Mommy Club that excludes men from co-ownership of parenting and the Daddy Pass that gives men the opt-out; in our outward identity as workers-only, such as when adults ask a child, "What do you want to be when you grow up?" and anticipate an answer that doesn't include "a parent" (especially from a boy), or when, as adults, we are forced to answer the question "What do you do?" at every reunion and cocktail party. In the boardroom, which still favors male leadership. On the golf course, where dads can freely play and moms can play if parental guilt doesn't get to them. In our culture's tenacious and narrow definitions of femininity and, especially, masculinity.

Some situations lend themselves more easily to breaking social barriers than others. Bruce, the family physician, had no trouble with colleagues thinking less of him for working part-time; his job was already kid-focused, and his desire to tend to his own children was not considered far-fetched. Brian, who worked as a public relations director for an art institute when his son was born, similarly felt no stares when he joined a female colleague in bringing his baby to work with him. ESP mothers also report that choosing a partner who is already an avowed feminist smoothes the way for equality. And ESP fathers who were raised to pitch in at home find it natural to continue in this manner when they have their own families—and even unthinkable not to do so.

But other families have a harder social road and are often trailblazers in their careers or at home. In these cases, it helps to have friends or colleagues who also desire equality and balance in some measure, if not full-out ESP. And so the last piece of advice that ESP couples give is to be on the lookout for your peers. Chat up that other dad at the story hour, reach out to the mom whose husband shows up with her at the pediatrician's office, or strike up a conversation with the couple next to you at your daughter's violin recital. Finding other ESP couples is not always easy (we've often wished they all wore T-shirts that advertised their family arrangements), but in our own quest for them, we have been rewarded with the real McCoys living only a couple blocks away from us in two directions. Chances are, you will have similar luck.

Whether or not you're able to surround yourself with a colony of like-minded ESP couples, you always have each other to lean on when social barriers arise. And your courage—to change the rules to fit your own happiness. And, of course, your wisdom—to notice the rules in the first place. Each barrier you break is a triumph, and one that is a bit less strong for the couples who will follow in your footsteps.

Conclusion

The Joy of Ownership

HALF THE WORK/ALL THE FUN

In the preceding chapters, we've had the pleasure of introducing you to a family model called equally shared parenting. We've described its two foundations, *equality* and *balance*, which support the sharing of four domains of a couple's life together—*childraising*, *breadwinning*, *housework*, and *self*. We have illustrated how dedication to these two foundations can strengthen a couple's resolve when pseudo-barriers such as *money* concerns or *social* expectations arise. And we've given you some examples of how individual ESP couples have built and now maintain this lifestyle. Along the way, we've offered ideas and philosophies that can help you build an ESP life for yourself, and some of the reasons why you might want to consider doing so.

Sometimes all the stars will align to make your equal partnership and balanced lives easy to achieve, and other times nothing will seem to go as planned. But ESP isn't simply a fair-weather lifestyle. We hope that we have been able to show you that its rewards make ESP worth holding on to through a few storms. A couple's ability to face inevitable difficulties and stay the course of their dreams comes from their deep inspiration to live this way. We call this *full ownership*.

In previous chapters, ownership has been mentioned in the context of owning our share of the work, responsibility, and power in our relationships; owning our competence in each domain; or owning the task of scheduling our work and leisure hours to balance with those of our partner. But the ownership we will explore in this conclusion is what brings equally shared parenting from an artificial parenting model to a joyful existence. Truly owning ESP is to internalize it—to take its essence, rather than its specifics, into who you are and how you live.

Internal ESP

Even with the best of intentions, the external logistics of ESP can come to a screeching halt for periods of any couple's life. "Our daycare is closing!" "My job is insane now; I'm on the road all the time since we've gone through a company merger." "My little hobby of playing in the band has gotten bigger than I ever dreamed it would; I'm booked solid playing gigs every night these days." "This book writing is taking up all our free time!" These are a few of the curveballs that life can throw into a couple's carefully orchestrated ESP arrangement (you might guess who said that last one). If ESP was defined only by its logistics, any one of these events could disqualify you, or possibly signal a more permanent end to your dreams. Fortunately, the core of ESP is far deeper.

As parents and as partners, we know that life brings each of us tough situations at one stage or another; ESP couples are hardly exempt. In fact, we have come to think of ESP couples as an extraordinary bunch of ordinary people. Although we didn't always mention their difficulties when describing the ESP couples highlighted in this book, we have introduced you to those who have battled through severe postpartum depression; are caring for a child with a crippling neurologic disorder, a live-in elderly parent, or twins; have gone through double adoptions, layoffs, and other financial stressors; have overcome ethnic and racial barriers; and possess widely diverging ideas about household cleanliness—to name a few of life's challenges. Nothing unusual here. But what is special about these parents is that we haven't yet met one who didn't remain committed to ESP for the long haul, who didn't believe it sustained them through the roughest days or frankly unequal periods, or who could think of a better way to live. They all own their individual, sometimes rough paths to getting and keeping their chosen life.

With every barrier you can get past, your ownership of ESP has a chance to grow. Every little step builds on the next and can secure your confidence for the next challenge. When you know how equality and balance feel—and you own ESP on a deeper level—you'll have the courage and conviction to make choices that will get you back on track as this becomes possible. And you'll be able to make decisions during those tough times that preserve the most important parts of your chosen life. A tough time for an ESP couple isn't a life sentence; you know where you're going, and your hope can remain alive no matter what.

The Youngest Owners

What legacy are we passing on to our children? Will the next generation own this life for themselves someday? Will they collectively finish the work of gender equality that we have started, or will they go a separate way entirely? We do not know these answers in any scientific way because they have not yet been studied. We know only a modicum more about the short-term effects of our chosen life on our kids. We know that involved fathers are good for children, through sound and diverse research.[7] We know that ESP is chosen by parents who, by and large, really want to live this way; we might conclude, therefore, that these parents are generally happy with their choice and can translate this into creating a happy home for their children. We can make other assumptions, too—that children can flourish by parents' dual involvement and can grow up with a solid sensibility from learning up-close two ways of handling life. Or that they will come to value nurturing, housework, and working for pay as equally important activities regardless of their gender. Or maybe that they will see the beauty of ESP in their parents' happiness, and be better armed than most young people at escaping tradition for themselves.

Several of the ESP couples we interviewed were gracious enough to arrange interviews for us with their teen or adult children, and we found their children to be delightfully expressive about their upbringing. They love the closeness of their relationships to both parents and feel that they "solidly know each of my parents as a person" and "have a real friendship with them." These grown-up ESP kids hope to create an equally shared parenting family structure when they have their own children, even as they watch some of their friends fall into traditional roles. But their plans go beyond just dreaming. Says one adult daughter, "ESP is not just an ideal for me—I lived it. It is not an exercise in imagination. I've seen the game plan in nitty-gritty detail. And I've got two parents who can remind me how it works if I just pick up the phone."

What about the drawbacks of such a childhood? One of our young interviewees summed it up this way: "I'd say the only problem is that when I go home to visit, I get told twice that there's smoked turkey in the fridge." We call this *doubletalk*, and it is a hazard of ESP—one we're willing to accept, however!

With so much still unknown about the scientific effects of equal sharing on our children, we can only continue to do what every parent strives for—give them our imperfect best every day and stay open to new ways to make this possible over time. Without a doubt, we're influencing them by our choice to coparent them, stay active in our dual moderate careers, jointly care for the home, and find time for ourselves and each other. What they do with this information—how they own it—will be up to them. Chances are, however, they will look back at their own childhood when they begin building their adult lives.

Full Ownership

Each time we meet a new ESP couple, we learn of a new reason to be passionate about this way of life and a new way of understanding others' motivations for tending it so carefully. Every couple has their own unique twist on how to share their lives, complete with their own challenges and triumphs. Some focus on equal and maximal time spent with their children, others concentrate on their career equality or maintaining the freedom that ESP brings to their career paths, while others build their center around a fun and varied life for each partner.

Among the couples you've been introduced to in this book are those who adore attachment parenting and those who are dubious of this notion, those who believe strongly in the benefits of breastfeeding for as long as possible and others who are adamant that nourishing and loving your baby well does not depend on the breast, those who believe no amount of daycare is tolerable and others who have found fantastic part- or full-time daycare arrangements, some who homeschool and others who would not consider such. Just as each couple in this book has created their own unique life, your ESP life will be another example of this splendid diversity. Your challenge now is to create your own unique brand of ESP.

At the end of many of our interviews, we often asked couples what ESP means to them. Let us finish with what just a few of these full owners of ESP said to us:

> The cornerstone of our marriage is the nightly conversations we have after the kids are in bed—about our lives, the kids. We can talk about anything because we both do everything. That we can share it all is what ESP is about for us.
>
> —*Melissa*

> ESP gives our family a clear identity—and not just one handed to us by society.
>
> —*Catherine*

We believe we are the authors of our own lives now. ESP is how we make this happen.

—Michelle

ESP is like bringing the concept of democracy into the family.

—David

For me, this is about the children. I'm going to cry now, but seeing the change in our son from being dependent on me as a baby to now, just a few years later, taking such strength from his relationship with his dad—that's what it's all about.

—Kitt

The joy and good feelings that come from a full life—family, travel, work, coworkers, our son—are pretty amazing. ESP gives us *both* this chance.

—Corinna

ESP is about making choices that reflect back your own personal highest quality of life. And it is our way of communicating with each other.

—Brian

ESP allows us to be a more legitimate form of ourselves.

—Annie

ESP gives me the sense that I'm doing the right thing. Nothing else would feel right for us.

—*Liz*

Everything I want to do and feel right now is possible because we're partners. ESP expresses my personal philosophy of aligning my life with how I want to feel.

—*Imari*

ESP is the epitome of equity between two humans who care about each other. I feel like I'm going to tell my kids this great story when they grow up about how we raised them together, and we'll be able to totally demystify gender roles for them. ESP is justice brought to childraising.

—*Cynthia*

For us, personally, ESP started as a way to ensure the intimacy and shared workload of an equal partnership (so deeply important to Amy) and to make our lives as adults and parents fun and balanced (the highest goal for Marc). Yet with each interview, we have added another layer of why we plan to stay the course.

A balanced life together as equal partners is a pretty lofty goal. In theory, it sounds dreamy—but in practice, well, outward sensibilities stop so many from thinking too hard about the idea, never mind reaching for or sustaining it long-term. Ah, but you now know the truth. Equally shared parenting is not easy; most things worth striving for aren't. But building and living a life in which you each share half the work is wholly possible—and a whole lot of fun. Our own road to finding out that it works has been deeply fulfilling, and equally shared parenting has been our greatest gift to each other and to ourselves. We give it to our children as well, in hopes that they will thrive through our joint involvement. We give it to you with our deepest wishes for your happiness. And we invite you to join with us as we extend the good news to all who want to know.

Additional Reading

There is *still* so much more to say! In this book, we have focused on the principles and practice of equally shared parenting—with an eye toward giving you what you need to consider, build, and tend it for your own. But that leaves out much of the history and research behind an egalitarian marriage with children, as well as related topics such as feminism, work-life balance, and money management that are of keen interest to many of us devoted to this lifestyle. Fortunately, many excellent books and online resources are available to complement this book's practical approach. Those we've found to be particularly useful are listed here, beginning with the ones we believe speak most directly to the ESP life. We also heartily welcome you to continue the discussion of equally shared parenting with us at our own website (www.equallysharedparenting.com), where you can read more couples' stories, news reports, and our blog, and review other tools to build and maintain this lifestyle.

Books Most Related to Equally Shared Parenting

Bem, Sandra Lipsitz. *An Unconventional Family*. New Haven, CT: Yale University Press, 1998. Fascinating personal story of an ESP family that is also devoted to feminism and gender neutrality.

Coltrane, Scott. *Family Man: Fatherhood, Housework and Gender Equity*. New York: Oxford University Press, 1996. Sociological discussion of shared parenting from the perspective of the father rather than the mother.

Deutsch, Francine. *Halving It All: How Equally Shared Parenting Works.* Cambridge, MA: Harvard University Press, 1999. The most comprehensive study of ESP, as gleaned from interviews with parents, with discussion of much of its philosophy and practicality.

Ehrensaft, Diane. *Parenting Together: Men and Women Sharing the Care of Their Children.* Chicago: University of Illinois Press, 1990. Intriguing discussion, based on interviews with ESP couples, about the emotional effects of this lifestyle on parents and on the children themselves.

Frank, Robert, and Kathryn E. Livingston. *Parenting Partners: How to Encourage Dads to Participate in the Daily Lives of Their Children.* New York: St. Martin's Griffin, 1999. Tips for each stage of your child's life, written by a family therapist and fatherhood-parenting researcher.

Gerson, Kathleen. *The Unfinished Revolution: How a New Generation Is Reshaping Family, Work, and Gender in America.* New York: Oxford University Press, 2009. Sociological study of the dreams of young men and women, describing how they desire egalitarian marriages but are not sure how to attain this ideal.

Greenspan, Stanley I., and Jacqueline Salmon. *The Four-Thirds Solution: Solving the Child-Care Crisis in America Today.* Cambridge, MA: Perseus, 2002. A book that touts ESP with each parent working two-thirds time as the solution for balanced families and healthy childraising.

Knudson-Martin, Carmen, and Anne Rankin Mahoney, ed. *Couples, Gender and Power: Creating Change in Intimate Relationships.* New York: Springer, 2009. Up-to-date academic exploration of gender and relationships that puts power differences at the crux of inequality.

Mahoney, Rhona. *Kidding Ourselves: Breadwinning, Babies, and Bargaining Power.* New York: Basic Books, 1995. Detailed, practical description of why women in our society end up with most of the housework and childraising tasks, and what to do about it.

Maschka, Kristin. *This Is Not How I Thought It Would Be: Remodeling Motherhood to Get the Lives We Want Today.* New York: Berkley, 2009. Passionate story of one couple's journey from tradition to ESP.

Meers, Sharon, and Joanna Strober. *Getting to 50/50: How Working Couples Can Have It All by Sharing It All, and Why It's Great for Your*

Marriage, Your Career, Your Kids . . . and You. New York: Bantam, 2009. Well researched guide to ESP for full-time earners.

Richards, Amy. *Opting In: Having a Child Without Losing Yourself.* New York: Farrar, Straus and Giroux, 2008. Call to women (and men) to take responsibility for creating the lives they want, with a discussion of some of the personal barriers to equal sharing.

Risman, Barbara J. *Gender Vertigo: American Families in Transition.* New Haven, CT: Yale University Press, 1998. A feminist look at gender and how it pervades all that we do, followed by an in-depth analysis of equally sharing couples and their children.

Schwartz, Pepper. *Love Between Equals: How Peer Marriage Really Works.* New York: Free Press, 1994. Beautiful ode to ESP that examines data on its benefits and challenges as compared to traditional and "near-peer" relationships. If you are contemplating ESP, this book will give you all the reasons to make it real.

Shields, Julie. *How to Avoid the Mommy Trap: A Roadmap for Sharing Parenting and Making It Work.* Sterling, VA: Capital Books, 2002. Excellent how-to book for creating ESP, primarily from a woman's perspective.

Books on Related Topics

Amato, Paul R., Alan Booth, David R Johnson, and Stacey J. Rogers. *Alone Together: How Marriage in America Is Changing.* Cambridge, MA: Harvard University Press, 2007.

Benko, Cathleen, and Ann Weisberg. *Mass Career Customization: Aligning the Workplace with Today's Nontraditional Workforce.* Cambridge, MA: Harvard Business School Press, 2007.

Bort, Julie, Aviva Pflock, and Devra Renner. *Mommy Guilt: Learn to Worry Less, Focus on What Matters Most, and Raise Happier Kids.* New York: AMACOM, 2005.

Cowan, Carolyn Pape, and Philip A. Cowan. *When Partners Become Parents: The Big Life Change for Couples.* New York: Lawrence Erlbaum Associates, 1999.

Dacyczyn, Amy. *The Complete Tightwad Gazette*. New York: Villard Books, 1998.

De Graaf, John, ed. *Take Back Your Time: Fighting Overwork and Time Poverty in America*. San Francisco: Berrett-Koehler, 2003.

Drago, Robert. *Striking a Balance: Work, Family, Life*. Boston: Dollars & Sense, 2007.

Fisher, Roger, William L. Ury, and Bruce Patton. *Getting to Yes: Negotiating Agreement Without Giving In*. New York: Penguin, 1991.

Friedan, Betty. *The Feminine Mystique*. New York: W. W. Norton, 1963.

Gilbert, Daniel. *Stumbling on Happiness*. New York: Knopf, 2006.

Hochschild, Arlie, and Anne Machung. *The Second Shift*. New York: Penguin, 2003.

Honoré, Carl. *In Praise of Slowness: Challenging the Cult of Speed*. New York: HarperOne, 2004.

Kossek, Ellen Ernst, and Brenda A. Lautsch. *CEO of Me: Creating a Life That Works in the Flexible Job Age*. Upper Saddle River, NJ: Wharton School Publishing, 2008.

Levine, James A., and Todd L. Pittinsky. *Working Fathers: New Strategies for Balancing Work and Family*. New York: Harcourt Brace, 1997.

Levine, Suzanne Braun. *Father Courage: What Happens When Men Put Family First*. New York: Harcourt, 2000.

Robin, Vicki, Joe Dominguez, and Monique Tilford. *Your Money or Your Life: 9 Steps to Transforming Your Relationship with Money and Achieving Financial Independence*. New York: Penguin, 2008.

Sennet, Richard. *The Craftsman*. New Haven, CT: Yale University Press, 2008.

Smith, Jeremy Adam. *The Daddy Shift: How Stay-at-Home Dads, Breadwinning Moms, and Shared Parenting Are Transforming the American Family*. Boston: Beacon Press, 2009.

Stone, Pamela. *Opting Out? Why Women Really Quit Careers and Head Home*. Berkeley, CA: University of California Press, 2007.

Warren, Elizabeth, and Amelia W. Tyagi. *The Two-Income Trap: Why Middle-Class Mothers and Fathers Are Going Broke.* New York: Basic Books, 2003.

Websites and Blogs

Babble: www.babble.com. Online parenting magazine written for both parents.

Campaign for a Commercial-Free Childhood: www.commercialexploitation.org. Eye-opening resource on commercial marketing to children.

Center for a New American Dream: www.newamericandream.org. Jam-packed resource for responsible consumption and conscious living, mixed with a whole lot of fun.

Center for WorkLife Law: www.worklifelaw.org. Nonprofit legal research and advocacy group devoted to identifying and preventing discriminatory employment practices against caregivers.

Council on Contemporary Families: www.contemporaryfamilies.org. Nonprofit organization of family researchers dedicated to enhancing the national conversation about family trends, including issues of gender.

Daddy Dialectic: www.daddy-dialectic.blogspot.com. Well-written blog by fathers who value egalitarian parenting.

Families and Work Institute: www.familiesandwork.org. Nonprofit research organization studying changes in the workplace, workforce, and family. Website include links to free downloads of many of the institute's reports.

FlexPaths: www.flexpaths.com. Web portal service for human resources staff, managers, business leaders, and employees who want to understand work flexibility options.

Get Rich Slowly: www.getrichslowly.org. Blog and money resource by J. D. Roth, a former cardboard box salesman who now has a big following in the world of sensible personal finance.

MomsRising and FamiliesRising: www.momsrising.org. Grassroots activist website aimed at improving corporate and government policy toward better parental leave, flexible work, children's healthcare, high-quality outside childcare, and fair wages for all.

Mothers Movement Online: www.mothersmovement.org. Noncommercial site focusing on cultural, economic, and political issues related to motherhood.

Simple Living Network: www.slnet.com. Resource for voluntary simplicity, in partnership with the book/program *Your Money or Your Life*.

Sloan Work and Family Research Network: www.wfnetwork.bc.edu. Huge collection of academic work on work/life and family issues.

Take Back Your Time: www.timeday.org. Website companion to the book *Take Back Your Time* and the initiative to challenge the routine lifestyle of overwork.

The Father Life: www.thefatherlife.com. Online magazine for fathers.

Thirdpath Institute: www.thirdpath.org. Nonprofit organization dedicated to reform, coaching, and education to make Shared Care (their term for ESP) possible.

WorkOptions: www.workoptions.com. Specializing in flexible and part-time work, with free tips to prepare for approaching your boss with the work schedule you want.

Acknowledgments

· ·

Grateful. In all our interviews with equally shared parenting couples, this was the answer they overwhelmingly gave in response to our question, "How do you feel about your lives?" It perfectly describes how we feel, as well, about being given this chance to describe such a life in book form. Gratitude in abundance.

When we set out to build a life of equality and balance for ourselves as new parents, we never imagined authoring a book. But life has a way of moving a soul along toward its destiny, in tiny steps that belie the full length of the journey taken. First came our astonishment at the lack of information available on an equal marriage with children, then the decision to launch a website, then connection after connection with other parents who believed in ESP as strongly as we do—and here we are.

Along the way, our passion for bringing equality and balance to family life has changed shape. What started as our own philosophy has become the burning torch of many—and our responsibility became doing justice to the lives of so many more pioneers and giving hope to those who wanted an equal partnership. This is no longer our show. And for this metamorphosis, we are forever grateful.

In particular, we owe enormous debts to Jennifer Cayea, our literary agent, who believed in ESP from the beginning and who calmed us down at each step into the strange new world of publishing. She came along at just the right time, and we'd like to think we returned the favor even a little bit when she took the leap into motherhood during our writing. "Equal sharing, my ass!" she did report saying to her husband during the early months—but hey, we can take credit for giving her the language with which to vent.

And to our editor, Maria Gagliano, for her spot-on vision and for shepherding our intentions into the right words when we needed this most. She understood from the beginning that this book is really about loving life—as a parent, a partner, a person—and made sure the fun showed. We are deeply thankful for her gentle and substantive guidance, her enthusiasm, and her partnership in making ESP come alive on these pages.

Our deepest admiration goes to the forty ESP couples who formally contributed to this book, and the many more who did so through informal sharing, whether they were specifically mentioned or not. Most of those described are identified by their real names and locations, although a few names have been changed upon request. Many are now our dear friends and have given us much to aspire to in our own daily lives; because of them, our priorities are better aligned with our truths. Special thanks for extra reading and guidance go to Angela and Dorea Vierling-Claassen, Michelle and Jim Franco, and Judy Kaye and Bruce Phillips.

To our families, who loved us through this project and always. Amy says: To my mom, Rachel, who embodies unconditional love and taught me not to fear living my own life, and my sister, Kathy (aka Snake— meant in the most loving way)—*sisko rakas* forever. Marc says: To my parents, Doris and Chanel, and my big loving family—especially Deb, Susan, Paula, Scott, and Kristen. You taught me that I could do anything—and cheered the loudest at my humble successes. Thank you for keeping our children happy and safe throughout this long writing process.

To Lisa Belkin, who gave us a voice and the confidence to use it. Thank you for believing in us and for recognizing the importance of our message. Thank you for insisting we were the ones to tell this tale and advising us to just start writing when we didn't know where to begin.

To our mentors and the giants of research in equally shared parenting—especially Francine Deutsch, Kathleen Gerson, Barbara Risman, and Pepper Schwartz. We bow before you, as humble reporters from the trenches, while you actually prove our lives. Undying gratitude goes to Francine Deutsch for her careful and honest review of our writing; your encouragement is like gold to us.

And most of all, to our children—sweet and wonderful Maia and Theo—the reasons why we've ventured into these lives at all. We are but borrowing your beautiful presence, and gratitude does not begin to explain the depth of our love for you.

Oh, and yes . . . here's to you, honey.

Endnotes

1 For an excellent description of young men's and women's concerns about family and work, see Kathleen Gerson, *The Unfinished Revolution: How a New Generation Is Reshaping Family, Work, and Gender in America*. New York: Oxford University Press, 2009.

2 Women without children typically earn a salary 10–15 percent more than women with children, even with similar education and work experience. For more information, read Jane Waldfogel, "Understanding the 'Family Gap' in Pay for Women with Children." *Journal of Economic Perspectives* 12 (1) (1998): 137–56. Or visit MomsRising at www.momsrising.org or the Families and Work Institute at www.familiesandwork.org.

3 For one such data source, see the National Survey of Families and Households (University of Wisconsin Center for Demography and Ecology) at www.ssc.wisc.edu/nsfh.

4 See Neil Chethik, *VoiceMale: What Husbands Really Think About Their Marriage, Their Wives, Sex, Housework, and Commitment.* New York: Simon & Schuster, 2008.

5 To read more about the concept of dual-income families and bankruptcy, see Elizabeth Warren and Amelia W. Tyagi, *The Two-Income Trap: Why Middle-Class Mothers and Fathers Are Going Broke.* New York: Basic Books, 2003.

6 For more statistics on marketing to children, visit the Judge

Baker Children's Center's Campaign for a Commercial-Free Childhood at www.commercialexploitation.org.

7 For a review of the influence of father involvement on children's outcomes, see Anna Sarkadi et al., "Fathers' Involvement and Children's Developmental Outcomes: A Systematic Review of Longitudinal Studies." *Acta Paediatrica* 97 (2) (2008): 153–58.

Index

About the Authors

....

Amy and Marc Vachon are the founders of EquallySharedParenting .com, the first dedicated resource for egalitarian parenting from the perspective of both genders. They have written their personal story of equally shared parenting in *One Big Happy Family*, an anthology by Rebecca Walker (Riverhead, 2009), their work has been covered by the *New York Times, Boston Globe, Guardian, Huffington Post, USA Today, The TODAY Show*, and other media, and they are active speakers at professional work/ life balance and family/marriage conferences. In their other lives, Amy is a clinical pharmacist in a management role, and Marc is an information technology specialist. Marc and Amy live in Watertown, Massachusetts, with their two children, ages seven and four.